What people are saying about Alexia Clonda...

Breathe Life
INTO YOUR INNER
CHAMPION

"What an amazing woman!! Her story resonated with me, her resilience to overcome her demons and health issues. Her mindset and determination, striving forward, never backing down on her goals are inspirational."

—Gabriella de'Zuna
Unleash Your Inner Champion

"Alexia's story in Mastery Unleashed is a profound journey of resilience, growth, and unyielding spirit. With each challenge, she not only overcomes but transforms, showing us that our deepest struggles can become our greatest sources of strength. This book is an inspiring reminder that no matter where you start, you can rise above any obstacle with the right mindset, tools, and the courage to keep going."

—Jesse Engelbrecht
SportMind Creator

"An amazing story of how hard work, perseverance, and a proper mindset can make anything possible."

—David Ames
Squash Coach

"In *Unleashing Your Inner Champion*, Alexia masterfully guides us through the tumultuous journey of life with an empowering message of perseverance and resilience. Her engaging writing style pulls you in from the very first page, making it feel like you're sharing a heartfelt conversation with a trusted friend.

Through her own inspiring narrative, Alexia shares the battles she has faced and the invaluable lessons she has learned along the way. Her ability to rise, time and again, when life knocks her down is nothing short of remarkable, and her insights on controlling our thoughts, feelings, words, and breath provide a powerful toolkit for anyone striving to overcome their own challenges.

This book is not just a story; it is a beacon of hope for all who read it. Alexia's words resonate deeply, reminding us that we all have the strength to unleash our inner champions. I wholeheartedly recommend *Unleashing Your Inner Champion* to anyone seeking inspiration and practical wisdom on their own journey toward resilience."

—Heather French
Unleashing Your Inner Champion

"*Mastery Unleashed* is an inspiring and essential read. Having played alongside Alex and witnessed her compete at an elite level in squash after overcoming devastating physical setbacks, I can personally attest to the effectiveness of her breathing techniques and mental reframing strategies. This blueprint, crafted by such a knowledgeable and motivational individual, offers invaluable insights to help anyone deepen their self-awareness and unlock their full potential."

—Nicole
Doctorate of Physical Therapy

Breathe Life INTO YOUR INNER CHAMPION

Alexia Clonda

www.alexiaclonda.com

Copyright © 2025 by Unleashed Publishing

All rights reserved. No portion of this book may be reproduced by mechanical, photographic, or electronic process, nor may it be stored in a retrieval system, transmitted in any form, or otherwise be copied for public use or private use without written permission of the copyright owner.

This book is a compilation of stories from numerous experts who have each contributed a chapter. It is designed to provide information and inspiration to our readers.

It is sold with the understanding that the publisher and the individual authors are not engaged in the rendering of psychological, legal, accounting, or other professional advice. The content and views in each chapter are the sole expression and opinion of its author and not necessarily the views of Christie Ruffino, Unleashed Publishing, or the Seven Figure Book Launch Joint Venture.

For more information, contact:
Unleashed Publishing
A division of Christie Lee LLC
1879 N. Neltnor Blvd. #316, West Chicago, IL 60185
www.ChristieRuffino.com

Printed in the United States of America

ISBN: 978-1-939794-36-9

Table of Contents

Dedication 1

The Power of a Story 3

Quote 5

Foreword 7

Introduction 9

Alexia Clonda: Unleashing Your Inner Champion 11

Christie Ruffino: Unleashed & Exposed 25

Jane Applegath: The Dawning 45

Carla Snyder: Where Do the Dreams Begin 61

Sue Mandell: Deserving Second Chances 71

Dr. Vasundhara (Vasu) Tolia: Art of Reinvention: A Journey from Healing Patients to Healing Minds 91

Shauna Van Mourik: You're Never Not Marketing: Stepping Into Your Authentic Power 105

Carla Lewis: Inside the Fishbowl: Navigating Leadership and Change 119

Shellie Seyfarth, PhD: Emerging from the Grind: Reclaiming a Life that Matters 131

Julie Caprera: Willing to Be Willing: A Leap of Faith and Love 143

Alisa Cooper: The Journey to Financial Freedom 159

Diane Murphy: Trailblazing Your Transformation: From
    Surviving to Thriving! 173

Tim Faris: Relationships Are All We Got 185

Mendee Williamson: Embracing Transformation 199

Dedication

I dedicate this book to all those who have struggled with illness, who have fought to find their place in this world, and who have ever been told they never could or never would. To those who have carried pain, doubt, guilt, or shame—who have felt unseen, unheard, or unworthy in a world that moves too fast to notice your quiet strength.

This book is for you—the fighters, the dreamers, the ones still standing when life has tried to break you. It's for every person who has ever wondered if they were enough.

You are stronger than you think. You are braver than you believe. And you are far more capable than you've ever been told.

Take back control of your breath, your body, and your life. Your vulnerability is not your weakness—it is your greatest strength. Asking for help does not make you small—it opens the door to healing, connection, and growth.

Never, ever give up. Even when it hurts. Even when it feels impossible. Because every breath you take is proof that you still have power. Power to change, power to heal, power to rise.

So, take that next breath—and breathe life into your inner champion.

With love, strength, belief, and faith,

Alexia Clonda

The Power of a Story

At the heart of every meaningful life is the impact we leave behind—the relationships we nurture and the legacy we create. Our journey is shaped by the unique experiences that define us, forming a one-of-a-kind blueprint that no one else can replicate. This personal blueprint, our own story, is our gift to the world, a unique pattern as distinct as a snowflake.

When embraced and shared, our story has the power to inspire, teach, and connect. If we don't have the courage to share it, that story is lost forever, along with the lessons and insights that could spark transformation in others. No one else can tell your story, and without it, the world misses out on a message that could alter perspectives, encourage others to push forward and create lasting change.

The ability to master our narrative is one of our greatest assets. True influence—whether in leadership, business, or community—lies in the way we craft and deliver our story. When we share the right story at the right time, we not only impact the lives of others; but we also expand the possibilities for our own lives. Each shared story can alter the trajectory of both the listener and the storyteller, fostering a ripple effect of growth and connection.

Whether launching a new venture, reviving a career, or rediscovering joy in life, storytelling empowers us to boldly step into the future. Embrace your story, for it holds the key to your next chapter. May it lead you to your ultimate purpose and inspire others along the way.

Power to you and the story only you can tell!

"Through resilience and determination, we can transform our greatest challenges into our greatest strengths and unleash the inner champion within us all."

Foreword

Every now and then, a story emerges that reminds us of what the human spirit is truly capable of. For me, as both a physician and a witness to Alexia Clonda's journey, hers is one such story.

From the very beginning, Alexia's path was marked with challenges most would never choose to face. Severe asthma, recurring infections, spinal surgery, and hip replacements at an unusually young age, the list of medical obstacles is long and daunting. Yet behind every diagnosis and every setback stood a woman who refused to be defined by her conditions. Where others might have seen limits, Alexia saw possibilities.

As a medical practitioner, I have cared for many patients who have survived illness. What sets Alexia apart is how she transformed survival into strength and strength into service. The discipline and persistence that carried her to the top of world squash were matched, if not exceeded, by her mental resilience. Adversity became her training ground, teaching her lessons about breath, mindset, and healing that no textbook could ever capture.

What makes Alexia's work so extraordinary is the way she has turned her personal battles into tools for others. Her methods are not theories; they are lived experiences refined into strategies that empower people of all ages to breathe more easily, think more clearly, and unlock their full potential. These techniques are as relevant to elite athletes as they are to anyone navigating the stress and demands of daily life.

Reading this book is like sitting with Alexia herself: you feel her warmth, her compassion, and her unwavering belief in your ability to rise above challenges. She does not speak from a pedestal but from the trenches of real struggle, offering wisdom born of hardship and hope.

It is with great admiration, both as a doctor and as someone privileged to know her, that I commend this work to you. May Alexia's story ignite courage within you, and may her methods guide you toward mastery not only in sport or career, but in the way you live and breathe each day.

Dr. Roberta Chow MD PhD

Introduction

I grew up being told what I couldn't do, this, I can't do that… With asthma so severe that it often felt like I was drowning in my own body, doctors warned me that playing sports could kill me. My childhood was filled with doctor's visits, long nights of struggle, and the feeling of being fragile in a world that seemed too big, too fast, and too harsh. And yet, even in those moments of fear and breathlessness, something deep inside me whispered, "There is more for you."

That voice became my lifeline. It led me to pick up a squash racket when everyone said I shouldn't. It carried me through countless battles with my health. It pushed me to believe when the odds said otherwise. And against all odds, it brought me to the top of my sport, making me the world's number one junior squash player, and later earning a world ranking of number five.

But what I want to share with you goes far beyond trophies and rankings. My real story is one of survival, of learning how to rise again after pain, trauma, surgeries, and heartbreak. And the greatest lesson I ever learned was this: your breath can save you, heal you, and transform you.

That is why I am sharing my story now. The truth is, the world feels very heavy right now. People are more stressed, anxious, and overwhelmed than ever. So many are silently suffering, just as I once did. And I know what it feels like to carry that weight and wonder if things will ever get better.

I don't want people to suffer the way I did. That's why I've made it my life's work to help others circumnavigate pain, to shorten their path, and to guide them toward strength, resilience, and healing—without having to hit rock bottom first. Helping people is my greatest joy. Watching someone reconnect with their own strength, seeing them expand and evolve into the best version of themselves—those are the moments that fill my heart.

This book is my love letter to anyone who feels broken, lost, or held back. It's not just about my journey, it's about yours. I share my lived experiences because I want you to see what's possible, to know you're not alone, and to inspire you to take action toward the life you deserve.

Like the many other courageous authors who have chosen to share their powerful stories with the world, my hope is that my story reminds you of this truth: you, too, have this power within you.

You don't have to just survive. You don't have to wait until life forces you to the edge. You can choose to breathe into your inner champion now; one breath, one choice, one step at a time.

This is your call to take that next step into healing, into growth, and into the life you were always meant to live.

With love, strength, belief, and faith,

Alexia Clonda

Alexia Clonda

Unleashing Your Inner Champion

There are four things you have total control of: how and what you think, feel and say, to yourself and others, and how you breathe.

At 18, I had just reached the pinnacle of my junior career. I was the number one junior in the world, a squash champion, and it only took four years. The title solidified my place in the sport and proved to me that I was more than my past and more than my asthma. I was a champion in every sense of the word. However, just when I thought I had finally outrun my demons, life threw me a curveball.

The doctor's words echoed in my ears like a thunderclap: "Give up squash, or you could die." I was 18, sitting on the cold, unforgiving examination table in a stark room that smelled of antiseptic and fear. My breath caught in my throat as I tried to process what he was saying. I felt like the walls were closing in, the room spinning around me. The one thing that had given me purpose, that had made me feel alive and strong—squash—was suddenly being ripped away from me.

"Your asthma is severe. It has now become life-threatening," he continued, his tone firm but compassionate. "Continuing to play at this level is incredibly dangerous. Your lungs can't handle it. You need to stop, or you're risking your life."

I could feel the tears welling up. My chest tightened as I struggled to breathe, not from asthma, but from the realization that everything I had worked for, everything I had sacrificed, could be lost in an instant. Squash wasn't just a game to me; it was my lifeline. It was how I had clawed my way out of the darkness of my childhood and how I had found strength and purpose.

I had made it to the top against all odds—a junior squash champion and the number 1 junior in the world despite my health issues. I wasn't ready to let that go. I couldn't. However, as the doctor's words sank in, the gravity of the situation hit me. If I didn't stop, I could die.

The reality was stark and unavoidable. This wasn't just about losing a game or a match; it was about losing my life.

In that moment, everything I thought I knew about myself and my future shattered into a million pieces. I felt a cold wave of despair wash over me. However, beneath it, there was something else—a flicker of defiance, a spark that refused to be extinguished. I wasn't ready to give up, not yet. I didn't know how. However, I knew that I had to find a way to keep fighting and to keep playing the game that had given me everything.

Little did I know, this was just the beginning of a journey that would test every limit, push every boundary, and ultimately redefine what it meant to be a fighter and a champion.

To understand why those words from the doctor hit me so hard, you have to go back to where it all began. My childhood wasn't what you'd call typical. I grew up in a home that was more broken than whole and dysfunctional. My mother already had four children before me, and then there were four more after me. My parents were war-torn refugees arriving in a new country with very little English and a very different life from what they knew. They were overwhelmed and struggling to cope. They did their best, putting a roof over our heads and food on the table. With a sick child on their hands(me), it was decided that I should go live with my grandmother, where I could get the necessary care and attention.

My grandmother's house was first a place of comfort and peace. It later turned into a place of confusion and fear. A relative who visited frequently took advantage of my vulnerability. As a result, I found myself trapped in a cycle of abuse that I was too young to understand, let alone escape. I was just a child. However, those experiences left deep scars, shaping my perception of the world as a hostile and unsafe place. I felt abandoned, unloved, and completely lost.

I was an overweight child with severe asthma. This set me apart from my peers and made me a target for teasing and bullying. I struggled to fit in at school, constantly aware of my breathlessness and the wheeze that followed me around like a shadow. I couldn't run and couldn't keep up with the other kids. Every physical activity was a painful reminder of my limitations. I felt like I was drowning, suffocated by my own body and by circumstances that seemed beyond my control.

However, everything changed when I was 13. I developed a crush on the school captain, who liked playing squash. They were everything I wasn't—confident, athletic, admired by everyone. I wanted to get closer to them and to find some way to be part of that world. That is when I decided to try squash. At first, it was just a silly attempt to impress them. However, from the moment I picked up that racket, something inside me shifted.

I was clumsy at first, fumbling with the racket and struggling to hit the ball. However, there was something exhilarating about it. For the first time in my life, I felt a flicker of something other than pain and fear—I felt possibility. My asthma still made it hard to breathe, and my weight slowed me down. However, I didn't care. I was determined to push through and to prove to myself that I wasn't just the sum of my weaknesses.

I then met my first coach. He was an elderly, overweight man who saw something in me that no one else had. He saw potential and a spark of talent that I didn't even know I had. He took me under his wing, gently pushing me and giving me the unwavering support and encouragement that I had always craved. Under his guidance, I began to improve. My body started to change. It became stronger and leaner. My asthma, while still a challenge, didn't seem like such an insurmountable obstacle anymore.

Squash became my escape and my sanctuary. On the court, I wasn't the scared, overweight kid with asthma. I was an athlete and a fighter. I poured all my pain and frustration into every swing and every sprint. I slowly began to see myself in a different light. I wasn't weak, and I wasn't a victim. I was strong, capable, and resilient. For the first time, I felt like I had control over something in my life. That something was me.

By the time I was 16, I was competing at a national level. The recognition and accolades that came with winning tournaments were thrilling. However, they were secondary to the sense of purpose and identity that I had found. Squash wasn't just a sport to me; it was a lifeline. It was the thing that had pulled me out of the darkness of my past and given me a reason to keep going.

However, the journey wasn't without its challenges. My asthma continued to be a constant battle. There were days when I could barely breathe. Every inhalation felt like I was sucking in shards of glass. I spent countless nights in hospitals, hooked up to machines that helped me breathe, wondering if I was pushing my body too far and if I was risking my life for a dream that might never come true. However, every time I thought about giving up, I remembered what it felt like to be that scared little girl hiding in the shadows. I knew I couldn't go back to that. I had come too far and fought too hard to let my body dictate what I could and couldn't do.

That dark moment stirred a determination from deep within me and a decision that would change the course of my life forever. I decided that I wasn't going to let my condition define me. I wasn't going to let fear dictate my future. I was going to fight. It wasn't just for my right to play but for my right to live life on my own terms.

That's exactly what I did. I sought out specialists, learned about alternative therapies, and found ways to manage my asthma. I reprogrammed my daily routines, my mindset, and even my diet, all in an effort to regain control over my body. It was a long, arduous journey filled with setbacks and challenges. However, I refused to give up.

In the process, I discovered something incredible. I discovered that I wasn't just fighting for myself. I was fighting for everyone who had ever been told they couldn't and for everyone who had ever been held back by circumstances beyond their control. I realized that my true purpose wasn't just to play squash. It was to inspire others and to show them that no matter what life throws at you and no matter how many times you're knocked down, you can always get back up.

This realization became the driving force behind everything I did. It wasn't just about me anymore; it was about something bigger. It was about using my story and my journey to help others find their own strength and their own purpose. It was about turning my pain into power and using that power to make a difference in the world.

Little did I know that this was just the beginning of a new chapter. It would take me on a journey of self-discovery, growth, and transformation that would ultimately lead me to my true calling.

After my retirement from professional squash at the age of 33, my asthma became uncontrollable once more. Even with more medication, the wheeze became constant, around the clock, nebulizing hourly. It was an intense reminder of my limitations and of the doctor's dire warning hanging over my head. Asthma could kill me.

At that moment, I learned on the news that a miracle cure for asthma had come out of Russia: a breathing technique.

A thought suddenly pierced through the haze of fatigue and frustration. *What if this is the miracle I was praying for?* I had spent years battling my condition. I was not going to let this asthma beat me. I would not let it dictate my every move and every breath. At that moment, I made a choice. I would not let asthma define my life or my future. I would fight. I would learn. I would adapt again.

The breathing technique became a daily ritual. My life for the next year revolved around learning how to breathe properly.

I learned this technique to strengthen my lungs and control my breath, gradually pushing my limits in a controlled, mindful way. I reprogrammed my daily self-talk, replacing fear and doubt with affirmations of strength and resilience. I also began to reprogram my feelings and beliefs, convincing myself that asthma was a challenge, not a curse. It was a battle that I could win with the right mindset and strategy.

However, it wasn't just about breathing. It was about transforming my entire approach to training and life. I overhauled my diet, focusing on foods that reduced inflammation and supported lung health. I embraced a rigorous fitness regime designed to build my endurance and stamina without pushing my lungs too far. I also learned the importance of rest and recovery, understanding that my body needed time to heal and strengthen between workouts.

These actions eventually not only improved my asthma but also reshaped my mindset. I became more resilient and more determined than ever to not just survive but thrive. I realized that overcoming asthma was about more than just physical endurance. It was about mental strength and emotional balance. These qualifications, earned through pain and perseverance, now empower me to help others who are facing their own battles. I can guide them. It is not just because of what I've read or learned. It is because I have lived it.

The decision to take control of my asthma was empowering. However, the journey that followed was not smooth. I initially saw glimmers of success. My breathing exercises began to make a difference, and I felt my lungs getting stronger. I started winning matches again, slowly reclaiming my place on the squash court. It was exhilarating to feel like I was finally making progress and like I was beating the odds. However, those early wins were just the beginning of a much harder path.

For every step forward, it seemed like there were two steps back. There were days when I woke up feeling invincible and ready to take on the world. However, there were also days when I could barely get out of bed. My chest was tight with asthma, and my body ached from the strains of spine and back injuries from pushing myself too hard and too fast. I thought that I could outpace my condition by sheer force of will. That mindset led to these injuries sidelining me for weeks at a time. It forced me to confront the limits of my body in the most painful way possible and, inevitably, surgery.

Navigating this journey alone was grueling and often discouraging. I didn't have a roadmap or a guide to show me the way, just trial and error, over and over again. I tried every possible treatment, from conventional medicine to alternative therapies. Some worked for a while. Others didn't work at all. I wasted time and money on programs that promised miracles but delivered nothing but disappointment. I hoped to find the magic pill or treatment to fix me.

The truth was that there was no magic. It just involved hard work, mistakes, and learning. I had to come to terms with the fact that my journey wasn't going to be a straight line. It was going to be messy, full of false starts and unexpected detours. I had to learn to be patient, to listen to my body, and to give it the time it needed to heal and adapt. I had to accept that failure was part of the process. It wasn't a sign that I was on the wrong path but a necessary step on the way to success.

One of the hardest lessons that I learned was the importance of asking for help. I was stubborn and determined to prove that I could do this on my own. However, the more I struggled, the more I realized that I couldn't go it alone. I reached out to others. I was being guided to explore my spirituality.

These connections made all the difference. They showed me that I wasn't alone and that there were others out there who understood what I was going through and were willing to help me navigate the weeds. They taught me that success wasn't just about being strong and determined. It was about being smart, knowing when to push and pull back, when to rely on my strength, and when to lean on others.

I see that those early struggles and countless failures were essential to my growth. They taught me resilience, patience, and the value of community.

They showed me that the path to success is rarely straightforward. It's okay to stumble as long as you keep getting back up. Most importantly, they prepared me to help others facing their own battles, to guide them through the weeds with the knowledge and empathy that can only come from experience.

I understand now that the journey is not always easy. However, it's always worth it. The key is to keep moving forward, even when the way is unclear. It is important to be open to learning, growing, evolving, and never be afraid to ask for help. That's the message and lesson that I carry with me.

As I journeyed through my struggles and setbacks, I began to realize that overcoming asthma, the many other illnesses and injuries, a spinal fusion surgery when I was just 29, chronic fatigue, four hip replacements, and three heart attacks was about more than just physical endurance. It was also a mental and emotional battle. To truly unleash my inner champion, I needed to reprogram not just my body but my mind and spirit. This transformation didn't happen overnight. However, it was through consistent effort and the development of a set of strategies that changed my life.

The first strategy was to **reprogram my daily self-talk**. I learned to replace the negative thoughts that often clouded my mind with affirmations of strength and resilience. Instead of focusing on what my body couldn't do, I began to celebrate what it could. Each day, I reminded myself that I was strong, capable, and worthy of success.

I then worked on **reprogramming my feelings and emotions.** I understood that the fear and anxiety that had accompanied my asthma for so long were not serving me. I started to cultivate feelings of gratitude and confidence, using mindfulness and meditation to shift my emotional state. This wasn't always easy. However, with practice, I found that I could choose how I wanted to feel, rather than being controlled by my circumstances.

Reprogramming my beliefs was another crucial step. I had to let go of the belief that asthma was a life sentence and a barrier that could never be overcome. I instead adopted a growth mindset, believing that with effort and determination, I could improve my health and achieve my goals. I began to see challenges as opportunities for growth rather than insurmountable obstacles.

Finally, I learned to **reprogram and retrain my breathing,** focusing on techniques that created heart and brain coherence, helping me to enter a flow state. This practice allowed me to remain calm and centered, even in the midst of intense competition or when facing my most severe asthma symptoms.

Here are four tips that helped me on my journey, and I hope they can also help you.

1. **Reprogram Your Self-Talk**

Replace negative thoughts with positive affirmations. Remind yourself of your strengths and capabilities every day.

2. **Shift Your Emotional State**

Use mindfulness and meditation to manage your emotions. Choose feelings of gratitude and confidence over fear and anxiety.

3. **Adopt an Open and Growth Mindset**

Believe in your ability to improve and grow. See challenges as opportunities rather than obstacles.

4. **Master Your Breathing**

Practice techniques that promote heart and brain coherence, allowing you to remain calm and focused under pressure.

These strategies not only helped me manage my asthma but transformed me into a stronger, more resilient person and entrepreneur. They taught me that with the right mindset and tools, we can all unleash our inner champion and achieve greatness, no matter the obstacles we face.

As I look back on my journey, I am filled with gratitude for every challenge and triumph that has shaped me into who I am. I have not only managed to conquer my asthma and many other health issues but have also built a life that aligns with my deepest passions and purpose. I wake up each day excited to empower others, helping them to unlock their potential and overcome their own obstacles, just as I did.

My vision now is to create a community where everyone feels empowered to unleash their inner champion. I believe that no matter what challenges you face—a health condition, personal setback, or a professional hurdle, you have the strength within you to rise above it. It is about finding the right tools, adopting the right mindset, and surrounding yourself with a supportive network that believes in your potential.

I invite you to reflect on your own journey. Have there been moments when you felt overwhelmed by your circumstances? Were there times when it seemed like life was asking too much of you? Know that you are not alone. We all have our battles. However, it's how we choose to fight and overcome them that defines who we are.

You have the power to change your narrative and to turn your struggles into strengths. You don't have to do it alone. I've walked this path, learned these lessons, and now I'm here to walk beside you on your journey. Together, we can reprogram your mindset, transform your beliefs, and cultivate the resilience needed to achieve your dreams.

Are you ready to take that step? Are you prepared to embrace your inner champion and live a life defined by courage and confidence? If so, I invite you to join me. Let's embark on this journey together. I promise, the best is yet to come.

Alexia Clonda

Alexia Clonda is a dynamic force in the worlds of elite athletics, breathing and mindset coaching, and spiritual healing. Alexia's life has been defined by extraordinary resilience, overcoming severe adversity to become a world-class squash player and a transformation coach. Born with chronic asthma and a distaste for sports due to the physical discomfort it caused, Alexia's early years were difficult. However, her story is not one of surrender but of relentless resilience, determination, and triumph.

Defying all odds, Alexia became the number one junior squash player in the world. This was an incredible achievement, given her asthma. Her journey did not stop there. In adulthood, she continued to defy expectations, reaching a world ranking of number five. She represented Australia at both the junior and professional levels, despite facing life-threatening health challenges.

Alexia's current mission as a coach is to guide others on their own journeys of personal growth and self-mastery. Drawing from her own experiences, she specializes in breathing, mindset, and spiritual coaching. Her unique approach goes beyond performance enhancement, tapping into the core of personal transformation. Through her holistic methods—encompassing the mind, body, emotions, and spirit—Alexia empowers individuals to unlock their inner strength, achieve clarity, and gain greater confidence and focus.

Alexia is more than a coach. She is an inspirational mentor who helps others redefine their potential. Her life proves that with the right mindset and resilience, adversity can become the fuel for success. If you are seeking a path to your best and highest self, Alexia Clonda is your guide to discovering the strength within and breaking through barriers to live your dreams.

Alexia Clonda
The Mind Breathing Edge
New York, NY
607-319-9161
mindbreathingdge@gmail.com
www.themindbreathingedge.com

Unlock Your Calm: A Free Guided Meditation for Grounding and Resetting

Feeling overwhelmed, scattered, or stuck in the chaos of daily life? It's time to pause, breathe, and reclaim your inner calm.

Discover *"Breathing for Calm, Grounding, and Resetting"*—a transformative guided meditation designed to center your mind, steady your emotions, and restore your sense of balance. Whether you're navigating stress, seeking clarity, or simply need a moment to reconnect, this powerful practice will leave you feeling refreshed, grounded, and ready to face the day.

What you'll experience:

- A step-by-step breathing technique to release tension and invite calm.
- Gentle guidance to ground yourself and feel more present.
- A powerful reset to align your mind, body, and spirit.

In just 7 minutes you will reset your energy and find your peace.

Claim your free download today and step into a more centered, grounded version of yourself. Because when you master your breath, you master your world.

www.themindbreathingedge.com

Christie Ruffino

Unleashed & Exposed

"True strength isn't found in the absence of struggle but in the courage to embrace our story, turn setbacks into purpose, and rise each time with even greater resilience."

—Christie Ruffino

The sun was melting into the horizon, painting the sky in strokes of tangerine and violet as I sat on the soft, golden sands of Cabo San Lucas. Around me, the waves rolled forward in a rhythmic pulse, pounding against the shore as if they, too, held secrets of loss and hope. Here, in this idyllic paradise, I should have felt alive, triumphant even. After all, I had earned this trip—my reward for grinding through a coaching program that promised to transform my business and life. However, as I watched the sun disappear, I didn't feel power, but something deeply hollow, like I was an outsider in my own success.

Every second spent there felt borrowed. It was a luxury I couldn't afford. The plane ticket that brought me here was bought with points from a maxed-out credit card, one where I struggled even to cover the minimum payment. I was carrying a heavy secret, one that tainted every wave and every color in the sunset. This was supposed to be a celebration. However, I was using the money for my mortgage payment just to be here, gambling on hope with the highest stakes—my home and my stability. I couldn't even tell if it was bravery or recklessness. I was treading water in an ocean of seven- and eight-figure earners, yet I felt like I was one misstep away from drowning in six figures of debt.

I sat there, feeling the sand slip between my toes, wondering, *What am I even doing here?* How could I guide others to success when my life felt like an illusion on the verge of collapse? I took a deep breath, trying to anchor myself, but the question lingered, haunting me like the shadows creeping over the beach. I was here to rewrite my story, yet I felt like I'd lost the pen entirely.

The memory of that trip still lingers, a reminder forever etched in my mind. Whenever I reflect on how I made it here or when I'm faced with a new challenge, I tell myself, "If I could overcome that, I can overcome anything." If I'm going to be one hundred percent transparent with you, that's just one of the many obstacles I've faced over the years. All of which, I believe, were allowed by God to make me stronger, more resilient, and more faithful. Yet... how many tests does one person need to build endurance?

During each of my seasons of struggle, I always felt like I was living two lives—one that people saw, where I was strong and successful, and the other, hidden really well, yet where I felt like an imposter. Every day, it sometimes felt like I was sinking further and further into a deep pit—with no light to be seen above. I had built my life around helping other women, guiding them to share their stories, reclaim their strength and purpose, and build thriving businesses. But was I the right person to do that? How could I stand in my power and guide others to step into the power of their story when I had yet to be vulnerable and share my most embarrassing story, as I will be doing in the words that follow?

Roots of Resilience

Growing up, my mother raised me on the principles of hard work and sacrifice. She was a single mom who held us together with sheer grit. Her actions were seared into my memory as the model of what it meant to survive. These early lessons became my *roots of resilience,* teaching me to hold my head high, to find pride in sacrifice, and that independence was everything. However, while I loved her deeply, I also learned that sometimes survival comes with a high cost, especially when it means carrying burdens alone and through sacrifice.

Following her example, I started my own family early. I married my high school sweetheart shortly after graduation, young and full of hope. I believed that we'd build a life that would grow stronger with each year. However, I quickly found that youth and love couldn't fill the gaps left by inexperience and unmet expectations. My husband and I dove into a business together, an auto repair shop, where I wore more hats than I could count—marketing, branding, bookkeeping, even payroll when the deductions had to be calculated manually every week for every employee.

By daybreak, I was up at 4:30, heading off to a part-time management job at UPS to cover the medical insurance we couldn't afford on our own, and by noon, I was back home to fulfill my motherly and wifely duties. We had two kids, and I had no intention of allowing their youth to be stained by our decisions, so I managed that role as if it were my only obligation. Once they went to bed at night, I would work on the daily business requirements. My life became a cycle: tending to the house, cooking, baking, dishes, laundry, yard work, play dates with their friends, sports, Girl Scout Leader, and staying on top of the shop's duties. While I was pouring my energy into every corner of our lives, he often came home to the couch, remote in one hand and a glass of Jack and Coke in the other, as if the day's work belonged solely to me. I felt my worth slipping away with every passing hour spent carrying the weight of two people's dreams.

The messages I received from that time still echo in my mind. I had become a workhorse, yet was still called lazy, fat, and stupid over and over, despite the fact that I was putting in twice the effort. At the time, I didn't recognize what was happening. I just worked harder to get his approval. I tried to be a better wife but kept failing. I remember looking in the mirror, the words sinking into me, wondering, *Was I really all those things?* In moments of clarity, I knew I wasn't; I was the one keeping things together. However, I believed the words enough to chip away at my self-worth. Eventually, when our marriage came to an end, I felt as though I'd been gutted—left with a blank slate but no idea how to fill it.

After the divorce, I was grateful to keep the house, but reality hit hard. With no formal resume and no financial support, I was truly on my own, with two children looking up to me for stability. Things are much different now. Today, spouses can't easily avoid their financial responsibility to support their children. However, at that time, he controlled both the business and the funds to hire an attorney, making sure I walked away with nothing. He wanted me to fail. However, I was determined to break free from the control he had over me. I could not let him win. I couldn't afford to throw a pity party and wallow in the injustice, letting my insecurities swallow me whole. I had to figure out how to create a life for us from scratch. My mind shifted to survival mode as I worked relentlessly to make ends meet. That is when I found my first calling in the power of community. More importantly, that is when I found God.

> *"Your past is not your fate, but can be the fuel for the future you were created to make."*
>
> —Christie Ruffino

Core of Conviction

Religion and church had never been a big part of my life. You could say I was a "Chreaster"—someone who only went to church on Christmas and Easter. As children, my brother and I were occasionally dragged along on those holidays by my dad's new wife. That was the extent of my church experience. I thought church was boring, unnecessary, and full of "weird" people. The one time we did accept an invitation from a neighbor to attend church, my husband's new car was hit and damaged in the parking lot by an unknown churchgoer—a mishap that promptly ended our attempts to return.

After the divorce, however, those same "weird" church neighbors began checking in on me. To one side of my house lived a pastor, and on the other, a church elder. In hindsight, I believe they were used by God to reach me. However, at the time, I only saw them as strangers with odd kindness. They'd drop by with cookies, books, Starbucks, or just to offer yet another invitation to join them one Sunday. *Why would complete strangers do nice things for me?* I would think. I was jaded and had come to believe everyone has an agenda. Eventually, their unwavering kindness softened me, and I realized that they genuinely cared. They loved on me with no ulterior motive and wanted me to know I wasn't alone.

Reluctantly, I accepted their invitation, and that "YES" transformed my life. I became one of those "weird" churchgoers I once dismissed. Over time, my faith grew from a small seed to a solid, unshakable foundation. I learned to rely on God more than my own abilities, discovering a strength far beyond myself. My faith is now my rock—*my core of conviction.* It's what grounds me, guides me, and shapes everything I do, empowering me to live with purpose and resilience.

Whatever storms I face, I know I stand firm, rooted in faith, and driven by a conviction that transcends doubt, fear, or failure. This conviction is my anchor and my greatest strength.

Branches of Belief

I'd always been naturally drawn to connecting people, creating relationships that could lift each other up. I saw the impact that came from bringing women together—women who, like me, had fought through trials they'd never asked for and came out stronger. These connections became my *branches of belief,* extending my faith in the power of community and mutual support. I, therefore, started building what would become a national networking organization. It was a space for women to support each other's dreams and businesses through referrals and collaboration. What started locally quickly grew, and within a few years and a lot of hard work, I created a thriving network that connected thousands of women across the country. Through this community, I saw firsthand how powerful it was for women to share their stories and turn their challenges into stepping stones.

Despite the success, the journey was anything but smooth. Life continued to throw curveballs my way. It felt like every time I reached a new peak, something would happen to pull me back down—reminding me of the fragility of all I had built. Financial struggles remained a constant undercurrent, and I was constantly "borrowing from Peter to pay Paul," barely keeping my head above water, even as I helped others rise. I still couldn't stop. I'd become the comeback kid, the woman who had no choice but to keep going because the alternative meant giving up everything.

Over time, I began coaching other women to share their stories through co-authored books, helping them use their stories as platforms for growth and visibility. Many of these women had overcome unimaginable challenges. Their voices remained silent until they were encouraged to be heard. As they found strength in their stories, I found strength in guiding them. However, even as I helped them craft their narratives of triumph, my own story felt like a crumbling façade.

Beyond the Façade

That's how I wound up in Cabo, on the edge of burnout, pushing forward yet feeling like a fraud. I had built a business of purpose, but my purpose felt constantly just out of reach, and my own finances were in such disarray that I could barely stay afloat. I was coaching women on visibility and success, yet every time I looked at my own life, it felt like success was slipping through my fingers. The beach in Cabo had become a place where I wrestled with my worth and my purpose, realizing that while I had spent years building a business around helping others find their power, I still hadn't fully claimed my own. I was standing beyond the façade I had so carefully constructed, confronting the parts of my story I had yet to own.

Back then, I thought my purpose was to help others rise. Over time, I came to understand that part of my purpose was also to share the rawness of my journey. Each setback and each layer of self-doubt and hardship was part of a story I needed to tell. I had to admit the truth: that sometimes, the person who helps others find their strength is the one who needs to heal the most.

Sitting in that mastermind and feeling the weight of my financial strain and hidden insecurities, I began to realize that my life's purpose wasn't just about helping others—it was about helping others while being honest about my own imperfect path.

It was in the brokenness of that moment that I found a new layer of strength, a deeper connection to my story that wasn't just about inspiring others but about showing up authentically, failures and all. I left Cabo not with the answers I thought I needed but with a deeper sense of truth. It was time to step fully into my story, to own not just the parts that were tidy and inspiring but also the parts that were messy, painful, and still unresolved. I knew that if I wanted to help others find their power, I first had to embrace every corner of my own journey, shadows and all.

My Next Bigger Story

The moment hit me like a flash of lightning on a quiet night—sudden, brilliant, and undeniable. Sitting alone one evening after that mastermind retreat, the answer was unveiled. I was at a crossroads, replaying the years of sacrifice, hustle, and compromise. I could see it all clearly: if I kept moving as I had, I would stay stuck in the endless loop of barely scraping by, telling other people how to find success while silently fearing my own future. The truth was stark—I had to change, or I would lose everything I'd worked for and everything I'd dreamed of.

The cost of staying the same was now greater than the fear of leaping into something new. This was no longer about trying to prove my worth; it was about redefining it from within. That night, I made a promise to myself: I would stop hiding and step fully into the purpose I had been circling all along. I would be brave and step into *my next bigger story*. I was not quite sure how that story would unfold, but I had a few ideas, and I embraced the process of figuring it out. While at times I was terrified of the pages of my story yet written, I was even more terrified of the struggle story loop continuing—forever.

> *"Insanity is doing the same thing over and over again and expecting different results."*
>
> —Albert Einstein

In the days following my lightbulb moment, I made a decision that would change everything: I would not allow my setbacks to define me. I began by facing my fears head-on, creating a plan to rebuild from the ground up. The first step was letting go of what was holding me back—the comfort of familiarity. I sold my house, put my most precious belongings in storage, and set out on a journey to start fresh with nothing more than my experience, determination, and faith.

I dove deeper into the work of transformation, studying and refining every aspect of my business model. I immersed myself in personal development and high-level coaching programs, pushing myself out of my comfort zone and applying what I learned. I discovered how to automate and streamline my processes, create high-impact offers, and scale sustainably—skills I knew would also be critical for my clients.

With each new skill gained, I became more equipped to guide others. I understood the pain of struggling in silence which strengthened my resolve to support my clients through their own transformative journeys. I had done the work, and I could now offer proven strategies to empower others to find their own path to success and freedom.

Every step taught me resilience, and every challenge became another qualification that would allow me to help others reach their goals. I didn't just learn how to grow a business; I learned how to do it with purpose, integrity, and a deep understanding of what it means to rise from the ashes. My journey wasn't just about survival—it was a masterclass in creating success from within, and it was exactly the foundation I needed to empower others to do the same.

Through the Thorns

Starting over felt invigorating, but it wasn't long before I realized that the path to rebuilding wasn't smooth—it was filled *through the thorns*, with obstacles that snagged and slowed me at every turn. My early days were marked by bursts of success and moments that gave me hope I was on the right path. Clients came in, sharing how my guidance transformed their confidence, their businesses, and even their lives. Each victory was met with new and unexpected challenges that threatened to pull me under.

I remember the first time I truly felt everything was coming together. I had secured a few high-paying clients, and their feedback was incredible. I could see the real impact my work was having on those I served. However, the reality of building and sustaining this business quickly proved far more complex than I had anticipated. On top of that, thoughts of reviving my networking organization after its post-COVID decline weighed heavily on me. I felt a responsibility to my members to bring it back to life. DPWN (Dynamic Professional Women's Network) felt like a third child—something I had nurtured from an embryonic idea into a thriving community. As much as I loved it, I found myself questioning if I still had the desire to regrow it back to the glory it once was.

My new business was finally starting to thrive, but I was doing it all myself. From client acquisition and event planning to handling finances and troubleshooting every issue, my days and nights blurred together. One week, I'd feel on top of the world, and the next, I'd be scrambling to make ends meet, questioning if I could sustain the workload alone. I thought I could manage it all. As I stretched myself thinner, cracks began to show. It became a cycle: I'd begin a new strategy, throw myself into it, and get a few new clients, but then find myself exhausted, wondering if I was truly making progress.

My mistakes were constant reminders of how much I still needed to learn. I started by investing heavily in marketing strategies I didn't fully understand. I poured tens of thousands into hiring coaches, hoping they'd help me crack the code, only to find myself with little to show for it. I also dove into trying flashy tools and software that promised to automate my business. However, without the knowledge to implement them correctly, they became more of a burden than a benefit. There were countless times I looked at my dwindling bank account and wondered if I'd made a mistake betting on myself.

Perhaps the hardest part was feeling isolated. Building a business can be lonely. While I was helping others find their voices, I felt as though mine was getting lost. I lacked the guidance of the right mentor, someone who could offer me a roadmap and save me from the costly trial-and-error path I was on. I'd sit down at my computer late at night, searching for answers online, piecing together advice from countless articles, videos, and books, hoping to find the one thing that would make everything click.

A New Venture Unfolds

Life wasn't just good—it was finally great! I was living the dream in sunny Florida, free from shoveling snow and braving Chicago's brutal, below-zero temperatures where every breath seemed to freeze my nostrils together like glue. My business was soaring, I was getting healthier from my daily pickleball activities, and I had rallied the existing DPWN Leadership Team, who were excited to help me rebuild.

A well-spoken friend then introduced me to a business venture that seemed promising. At the time, I was so eager for success that I dove in big. I trusted him as he shared how his previous experiences with this venture had yielded him hundreds of thousands of dollars. He personally knew the company owner, who had a proven track record in this field. While I didn't have the capital he did to invest, I had the proceeds of my house sale, and I wanted to believe I was finally on the brink of something big, something that would propel my life forward and forever lift the weight of financial uncertainty. I was excited to see this *new venture unfold!*

I did research on the company and the principals involved. I had the investment agreement reviewed and all seemed in order. I spoke with my friend several times with questions and the VP of Sales. They both assured me that I was in good hands. In fact, I was getting a special opportunity, he said, with an extra "Waterfall Payment" in addition to the quarterly dividends that was only offered to the friends and family of the company executives, while all others only received the dividend payments. My final step was to pray about the decision and see how God would counsel me to proceed. I don't get audible words from God, but find that He speaks to me through dreams. Although I don't typically remember my dreams, each time I pray about something critical, I often wake up with a vibrant dream memory—a clear awareness of what I believe He wants me to know. That morning, I woke up after seeing my life filled with calm, joy, and of a family experience only money could buy, so I said, "YES."

Over the next few months, things flowed along smoothly. I received my dividend payments as scheduled. The relationship with my friend continued as we discussed my frustrations with online dating and his frustrations with his new girlfriend and her daughter. I was even in a phone text chain with him and the company executives, getting frequent updates on the project's progress and future returns. There were no red flags that gave me any indication about what was about to happen.

When Trust Turns to Betrayal

Eight months into this venture, my whole life crumbled into dust literally overnight. When trust *turns to betrayal,* the impact is devastating. My next dividend payment didn't arrive as planned, and every attempt to communicate this oversight was ignored. I reached out to my friend, but he was also ghosting me. Just that fast, I went from feeling on top of the world to understanding why so many people believed that jumping out of a highrise building was their only option after the stock market crash of 1929. No, I never entertained the idea, but with my life savings gone, I was overcome with such a sense of dread that I found it hard to pray my way out of it.

I felt betrayed—not only by the friend who'd introduced me to this investment but also by myself for trusting. It was a harsh lesson! It left me reeling, yet it reminded me of the importance of discernment and drew me closer to God, leaning on His provision in all ways.

> *"Look at the birds of the air, for they neither sow nor reap nor gather into barns; yet your heavenly Father feeds them. Are you not of more value than they?"*
>
> —Matthew 6:26

Despite this setback, I tried to keep moving forward, determined to make things work. I truly believe that every one of my failures sharpened my resolve and brought new insights, but the cost was always very high, both financially and emotionally. I found myself forced to confront my weaknesses, to learn skills I hadn't anticipated needing, and to accept that, without guidance, I was bound to make additional mistakes that could be avoided.

My coaching business was still doing well, but I had made significant growth decisions based on the expected date for my investment return and the anticipated waterfall bonus payment. When that didn't come through as planned, I faced a series of tough choices: I let go of my dream to rebuild DPWN, put my top-rated podcast on hiatus, and canceled a business cruise I'd been planning to host in 2025. It felt like everything I'd built was slipping away. I spiraled into a season of deep depression, feeling like an utter failure and an even bigger imposter. I was ready to give up and get a regular job. My prayers grew more desperate, but it felt like God was ghosting me too. I was pleading for help, but all I heard in response were crickets.

A Divine Alliance

A few months later, I woke up on a Saturday morning after finally hearing from God in another dream. I had given up on asking and was resigned to His silence. However, that morning, the message came through without my desperate pleas. In the dream, my current business partner appeared as the person who held the answers I'd been seeking. At the time, I barely knew him, but what did I have to lose? I decided to reach out and see what this *divine alliance* was all about.

To my surprise, he replied almost immediately. Within a few hours, we were on a call. I didn't even know what to ask him. I just knew I was meant to connect with him. I knew a bit about his story—how he had made and lost millions several times over—and thought maybe he could share some wisdom about resilience and bouncing back. Perhaps, I hoped, he could help me find a way to start over, just as he had done so many times.

What unfolded after that initial conversation became an unexpected opportunity to revive one of his former businesses that had been dormant for some time. With my publishing background, it felt like a perfect fit, and the program would offer invaluable resources and support for both my current and future clients. I couldn't help but be skeptical: *What's the catch? Could I trust this man?* My track record hadn't been great, but I wondered, *Why would I be led to him if this, too, was going to end badly?* I discussed it with a friend, and together we weighed the pros and cons. Then, just a few days later, I took a deep breath, said "YES" once again, and got to work.

*"Success does not necessarily mean to be rich or famous,
but to make an impact in the lives of those we were created to serve."*

—Christie Ruffino

Through it all, I realized how crucial it was to have a support system and to have someone with experience guiding the way. I saw firsthand how going alone—believing I had to figure it all out myself—wasn't the way to build something sustainable. It was time-consuming, costly, and at times, disheartening. My journey wasn't just about building a business; it was about finding the courage to ask for help, invest in knowledge, and learn from others who had walked the path before me.

Looking back, those struggles became the foundation of my expertise. I didn't just read about success—I earned it through each mistake, every failed investment, and every sleepless night spent wrestling with doubt. I can now guide others not just from a place of theory but from hard-won experience. I understand the value of a clear roadmap, and I am passionate about sparing others from the costly, painful path that I traveled alone. I now see that every setback prepared me to be the guide I wished I'd had earlier, ready to help others navigate their own journeys with greater clarity and confidence.

The *Seven Figure Book Launch Program* is designed to help frustrated entrepreneurs scale from six to seven figures, because they're sick and tired of inconsistent cash flow and not having the impact they desire. We help them enroll more clients with ease into a high-ticket group program that leverages their time and increases their income, and then scale with a great business book, conversion strategies, and automations. Best of all, our unique risk-reversal investment model fosters a sense of shared responsibility because our clients only pay us as we guide them to achieve specific revenue milestones, ensuring that they are on track to build a seven-figure business within two years or less.

Strategies to Profitize Your Purpose

The journey through struggle and growth became my personal forge, refining me with each challenge. I learned that true success wasn't just about survival but about harnessing each experience to build something stronger. Out of this process, I developed a framework—my EPIC strategy—that I now use to guide others in achieving their own transformations. These strategies aren't just lessons; they're the pillars that transformed me into the empowered entrepreneur I am today.

Strategy 1: Embrace Your Story

Our stories are our most powerful assets. Each one is a series of lessons uniquely crafted to shape us for what comes next. Embracing our story means accepting every chapter—both the triumphs and the trials—as essential steps in our growth. When we allow ourselves to fully own our journey, flaws and all, we unlock a new level of self-awareness, wisdom, and strength that equips us to step into the next, better version of ourselves.

By embracing my story, I found not just the ability to help others, but the courage to trust that each part of my past served a purpose. This acceptance taught me that vulnerability isn't a weakness, it's a bridge to genuine connection, inviting others to see not just where we are, but where we've come from. By exposing our truth and accepting the fullness of our story, we gain the resilience and insights needed to unleash our true brilliance with confidence. We become better prepared for the newer and better stories we're meant to create. Embracing our journey allows us to expand, to grow into more authentic and empowered versions of ourselves, ready to write our next chapter with clarity and purpose.

Strategy 2: Profitize Your Purpose

Our purpose is more than just a calling—it's what we were created to do. When we align our business with that purpose, it becomes a powerful force for success. Purpose alone may ignite passion. However, to build a sustainable, thriving business, purpose needs to be paired with intention and strategy. Rather than wasting time and energy on a career path that doesn't resonate, a purpose-driven business allows us to channel our talents, values, and strengths into something that naturally expands and flourishes.

When I shifted my focus to turn my purpose into a profitable model, everything changed. By building high-value offerings around what I was meant to do, I found I could serve deeply and sustainably. Purpose-driven work isn't just rewarding—it becomes magnetic, drawing in the right clients, opportunities, and growth, because it aligns with who we truly are. This alignment doesn't just make the work fulfilling; it creates a foundation for real, lasting success not only doing what we love, but doing what we're meant to do.

By following our purpose, we build something much greater than a business; we build a legacy of impact. Every decision, every action, becomes infused with meaning, naturally guiding us toward the next right step.

Strategy 3: Increase Your Impact

To truly expand my reach without risking burnout, I leaned heavily into systems and automation. By implementing automated processes for client onboarding, scheduling, and follow-up, I created a business that could grow sustainably. These systems allowed me to maintain quality and consistency, ensuring that every client received the same level of service and care, even as my business scaled.

Automation freed up my time from repetitive tasks, allowing me to focus on high-impact areas like strategy and client connection. With these tools, I could increase my capacity to serve, while preserving the personal touch that defines my brand. Systems and automation enabled me to expand my impact thoughtfully, balancing growth with energy and efficiency. They're not just tools—they're essential to creating a business that thrives without sacrificing quality or well-being.

Strategy 4: Collaborate to Accelerate

Collaboration quickly became a cornerstone for my growth and success. I sought out like-minded partners who shared my values and vision, building a network of individuals and businesses aligned with my purpose. These partnerships allowed us to pool our strengths, exchange insights, and support each other's growth. By working together, we created a community of support that made reaching new audiences not only possible but far more impactful than if I had gone it alone.

Beyond expanding my reach, collaboration enabled me to serve clients more effectively. Each partner brought unique expertise, allowing us to provide a richer, more comprehensive experience for those we served. We reached audiences together we couldn't have accessed individually, opening doors to new opportunities and helping each other grow in ways we hadn't imagined. In the process, collaboration proved to be more than a strategy; it was a powerful accelerator that multiplied my impact and reinforced the value of building meaningful connections.

> *"There is power in standing inside a vision and generating life from that possible future."*

—Christie Ruffino

I'm now living the life I once dreamed of, fueled by purpose, resilience, and alignment with my values. My journey has brought me here—not just to a place of success, but to a place of fulfillment, where every part of my story fuels my work and brings value to others. I get to wake up each day with clarity, helping others transform their stories, profitize their purpose, and build lives that reflect their deepest dreams. This work, rooted in my own struggles and triumphs, is what drives me to continue expanding my impact.

I didn't get here alone, and neither should you. If parts of my story resonate with you—the ups and downs, the relentless pursuit of something greater—you know that the journey doesn't have to be walked alone. Your purpose deserves a framework, a strategy that aligns with your passion while leading to lasting success. Imagine what's possible when you harness the full power of your story and create a life built around it.

That's why I created the *Profitize Your Program Action Guide*—a step-by-step tool designed to help you fill your group coaching program and make more money with powerful strategies most coaches don't want you to know about. This guide offers the same insights and strategies that I've used to build a life I love, serving both my dreams and my clients.

If you're ready to bring your story to life in a way that profits both you and the people you're meant to serve, I invite you to take the next step.

Let's make your journey epic, TOGETHER.

To read Christie's full story go to www.UnleashedandExposed.com

Christie Ruffino

Purpose Profitization™ Strategist

Christie Ruffino isn't just a serial entrepreneur; she's a narrative ninja and a speed-loving strategist who turns entrepreneurs into empowered brand heroes. With a sparkling career as a business coach, podcast host, international speaker, and best-selling author of 18 books, Christie knows a thing or two about captivating an audience.

After three decades in business, creating three six-figure businesses, and empowering over three thousand women to boost their business revenues, Christie has mastered the art of blending STORY, SYSTEMS, & COMMUNITY to help more people and make more money. She's not just a coach; she's a Purpose Profitization™ guru who guides her clients through the mystical arts of packaging their expertise into a high-impact offer that guarantees success and a great business book that skyrockets their income, so they can enjoy a seven-figure business that lights them up, guaranteed.

When she's not crafting killer strategies or leading the charge on her Harley at triple-digit speeds (because who needs skydiving when you have horsepower?), Christie is a self-proclaimed "serial smart ass." She's also a devoted grandma to the two most adorable grandkids on the planet and has an extensive photo collection to prove it!

Christie Ruffino
Mastery Unleashed Coaching
630-336-3773
Christie@ChristieRuffino.com
www.ChristieRuffino.com

Profitize Your Program™ Action Guide

Discover how to attract more clients, create a greater impact in their lives, and banish inconsistent cash flow from your coaching business FOREVER. This comprehensive guide provides proven strategies to help you build a thriving coaching practice that consistently generates income and makes a meaningful difference in your clients' lives.

https://bit.ly/pypmu

Jane Applegath

The Dawning

> "Behind the darkness there is the light,
> Run from it now or stay and fight.
> Embrace your power in this dawn,
> Before death declares it's forever gone."
>
> —Jane Applegath

The Fall

There is a misconception that our shadows are what we fear, when it is the power of our light that scares us most.

I am accustomed to living in overdrive. For years, I was a goal-getter, striving for the top rank, accolades, and praise—no matter the "soul-sucking" price. I stunned everyone when I walked away from a lucrative career as a top-ranking financial advisor. Money can be a seductive manipulator. When I became its servant, I knew it was time to leave. That's when I became an entrepreneur. My epic journey was only just beginning.

Embrace your light when the darkness wanes, for the dawn renews where courage reigns.

My stomach tightened as I closed the door to the garage that was the business warehouse. A space that once held the promise of success now stands empty and silent—a tomb for a dream that barely saw the light of day. Doubt screams from the shadows:

*"What happened to the woman who believed in impossible dreams?"
it taunted. "Where's the fire of determination that fueled your
soul for so long?"*

I clench my fists seeking to hang onto the dreamer that is slipping away like sand through my fingers. What the blip do I do now, my thoughts shout. There is no answer.

"Our greatest glory is not in never falling, but in rising every time we fall."

—Confucius

Where Shadows Fall
Beware of the Whispers of Ruin

Years pass. The start-up is a slow-fading memory. But there are echoes of fear all around.

And then; the recession strikes like a tidal wave. The once vibrant city we live in is a ghost town. Fear hangs in the air like a thick fog, choking the hope out of every tomorrow.

My heart lurches every time the phone rings. The bill collectors are like vultures, picking apart what little remains. All I can do is let the phone ring, while the predators dismantled our lives.

An internal war wages between the anxiety and chilling hopelessness that have taken root in my soul. The arena of my mind is full of shadows that fight to overtake my will.

So, I seek the one refuge I know all too well: the "Wall" that guards my heart. It's my shield against a world I'm convinced seeks to break me. Behind the "Wall" is the emptiness I chase. It is the void of nothingness that I crave.

Science says how we see ourselves shapes the way we move through the world, often without us even realizing it. Our self-perception always influences how we present ourselves, the choices we make, and what we believe we're capable of achieving.

Walking away from the hollow shell that was once a home, now claimed by the bank, I feel shattered. I've become friends with defeat and heartache. It wasn't just the move—it was another door closing as if I were abandoning the fearless creator, the relentless achiever, the woman who once believed she could conquer the world.

And yet, despite my efforts to shut every thought down, a voice whispers…

"What's a worse fate, dreaming of conquering mountains or not dreaming at all? This isn't the end. It's only the beginning."

The words are faint, almost imperceptible to the roar of grief, but they are there—waiting for the day I would listen.

"You are not here to concede to the little girl you're trying to protect. You are here to fight for the powerful woman you are here to be."

Nothing Stays the Same Forever
Even Fortresses Crack

Mortality is a sobering thought. Even though we know it will find us all, it collides with the very essence of our being. When it strikes without warning, it's crushing.

The recession had passed; we had survived. Then tragedy hit with unforgiving force. Three family members were gone, their absence a gaping wound in my heart.

The fear builds like a storm within me as my fortress, the "Wall," crumbles into dust. The gateway to my heart is now wide open, and an inner tsunami slams into me with all its force.

Doomed emotions threatened to rip a hole in my chest. Mounting anxiety travels through me at warp speed, consuming every fiber of my being until it's all I can feel. There's no misconception in my mind: I'm a hunted animal with no escape.

Out of the depths of my memory, I hear this unforgettable quote in my head:

> "Death whispered; Live for I am coming!"
>
> —Oliver Wendell Holmes Jr.

Confidence, once my greatest asset, was now a distant memory. I feel paralyzed by dread, every nerve in my body on edge, waiting for the next blow to hit. I had spent countless years building a stronghold around my heart, but now that fortress was gone, and the dark shadows surrounded me, trapping me in like a caged animal.

The voice inside me thunders…

"How long will you remain the numb woman you created to simply feel all right? When roars of another woman keep you up at night? What are you waiting for? What are you aching for? Maybe you're the light that you've been looking for."

To Leave the Comfort of the Known
Is to Dare to Believe in the Unknown

> *"I've been through some terrible things in my life, some of which actually happened."*
>
> —Mark Twain

Have you ever felt that your life was unfolding like pages out of a bizarre comic book series? It is a strange mix of horror, science-fiction, drama, and delusion. I don't know about you, but it was not the role I would have chosen to star in, let alone be in.

I had come ready to fight, and amid my battle, I had lost my "Armor;" that shield of protection I called the "Wall" had vanished. I felt exposed and vulnerable. Do you know this feeling?

I have learned that we are confined only by the walls we fabricate from the ashes of our limiting beliefs and records of the past. These walls may be our gatekeepers, but they will not open to allow us to fly. Our strength does not come from building walls. It comes from tearing them down.

In that realization, I heard the unspoken words in my head...

"You are not the darkness you fought. You are the light that refuses to surrender. Choose! Die from the fear that will crush you.
Or live by the courage that will empower you.
Say, YES, to the Epic Woman that's been waiting for you all your life."

There, amidst the debris of my jumbled thoughts, was the light I'd been running from. The spark of resilience that remained, waiting for the day it would ignite into a flame that would guide me—and others—out of the darkness.

Liberate the Ordinary for the Extraordinary
For Both Cannot Survive Together

"She remembered who she was, and the game changed."

—Lalah Delia

When it feels like you're anchored at the crossroads of routine and rebellion, longing for the extraordinary while tethered to the ordinary, you know something's got to give.

It's a hair-raising experience these things we call rock bottom, the dark night of the soul, and that unscheduled trip to hell and back.

There are no instructions or GPS coordinates to navigate the wild intersection between the light and the darkness that you never gave permission to blow your mind to smithereens.

What I can tell is crossing the threshold in the prime of your life changes everything. It's a wake-up call to stop pretending that we can go about "life as usual."

Our lives are taking place in the here and now. In this realm, they are the most time-critical and precious things we have been gifted. So, ask yourself, as I have, what will my life story be?

> *"Do not be satisfied with the stories that come before you.*
> *Unfold your own myth."*
>
> —Rumi

Alchemize Your Own Rebirth

> *"A woman who has been to hell and back and keeps her heart pure,*
> *her soul intact, and her spirit soaring, isn't a woman.*
> *She's an alchemist. She's magic."*
>
> —@femalebosssuccess

It's time to defy the norm, rewrite the rules, adopt a new mindset, and reclaim life like never before. It's time to commit to guess who? You. Because at the end of it all, who wants their tombstone to read: "What the f*@* happened?"

Maturity, how you define it, is THE REASON you get to RISE to have everything you want, NOT the reason you can't. Whether you're currently navigating business, an awesome reinvention, or the fruitful integration of both, I'm here to tell you it's not a distant dream.

We all have the power to declare, "This is not how my story will end. This is how it begins."

So, I ask you to take a good look at who you really are, as I have done over the past few decades. Reigniting your light is about getting reconnected to the extraordinary woman you already are.

> *Listen to your inner voice, for therein lies the dreamer*
> *who wants to light your Soul on Fire.*

Our Greatest Story is Our Comeback Story

> *Every comeback is infinitely stronger than any setback.*

At some point, every woman who allows herself to become aware and listen discovers that she is not here to settle for the end in sight. She is here to gear up for no end in sight.

Over the years, I have masterfully adapted to the art of reinvention. As a previous award-winning financial advisor, entrepreneur, television producer, scriptwriter, yoga instructor, VUCAMAX leadership coach, and now a global podcaster, I've learned that our future is never a foregone conclusion.

It's said that we often feel tired, not because we've done too much, but because we've done too little of what sparks a light in us. It's something I have felt throughout my career choices. I was successful and respected, yet something was missing. Can you relate?

What I've discovered through my continuous learning is that growth is not an accident, nor is it where comfort resides. However, I know it is where the magic happens. Whether you choose to believe it or not, our experiences are never spontaneous. They are intended destinations fated to us as reminders of the extraordinary, resilient women we are here to be.

The Roar of Fire Begins with a Spark
Unleashing the Transformative Power of Your Voice

Your voice has the power to awaken your senses, elevate action, inspire change, ignite influence, build community, and cultivate epic legacy and leadership. I know this because I've experienced it firsthand.

I didn't start my video podcast, titled the Epic Vision Zone, until I was in my 50s. Despite my career experiences, I'd never been in front of a camera before. I also didn't have an Instagram account, an email list, or any kind of reputation when I started. I had no marketing budget or branding, but what I did have was my steely fifty-something determination, carrying a fiery resolve to make my voice matter to others as much as it did to me.

Believe me when I tell you that finding your voice is transformative. It's your authentic expressiveness, the cornerstone of your identity, and the essence of how others perceive and connect with you. It begins on the inside, and with courage, confidence, skill, and practice, it can reach the world at large.

Your voice is your power source to manifest who you came here to be. Whether it's your "Inner Voice" or your "Public Voice," it is the source that can liberate the marvel of your extraordinary presence. The key is to be present enough to recognize its genius.

If this sounds amazing to you, then it's what I want for you. You are not here to live a mundane existence. You are here to live in jaw-dropping awe of your EPIC life's story.

Start with these Epic Igniters

1. Unleash Your Voice: Unleash Your Power

"The way we choose to see the world creates the world we see."

—Barry Neil Kaufman

Here's some wild science for you. Our reality is responding and shaping itself according to our consciousness. This is the quantum law of being, one lesson from VUCAMAX, an acronym for Vision, Understanding, Clarity, and Adaptability.

It is hard to believe that everything starts with the voice of YOU. The words you tell yourself are the architects of your reality. Negative self-talk and limiting beliefs, when at the core of your inner broadcast, are the roadblocks that hold you back.

Your inner "script" impacts your life both consciously and subconsciously. Empowering it to work in your favor is paramount to reclaiming a growth mindset. VUCAMAX teaches us to "flip-the-script" to create an inner dialogue that celebrates our strengths and potential.

Over time, this practice will prime your mind and energy with a profound sense of purpose, and you will begin to align with the "starring" role you are here to experience. Bottom line: Tune your voice to become your greatest source of inspiration, love, and celebration.

Actionable Step

Start a daily practice of positive affirmations. Write down three empowering statements about yourself, then videotape them on your phone. Play them back every morning and night. Replay the video whenever you feel stuck. This simple exercise can be the first step toward transforming your inner narrative. Have fun with it.

2. **Awaken to Awareness: Flip the Switch**

"Awareness is the great agent of change."

—Eckhart Tolle

How often do you think about what you're thinking about? How often do you consider that there is a "program" repeating itself in your head? Most of our thoughts, reactions, habits, emotions, and behaviors are on autopilot, recycling negative patterns that drain our energy. It's like a "bad playlist" that plunges us into a lousy mood or, worse, a lousy life. Are you with me?

By becoming aware of these patterns, you begin to understand what's "clogging the drain" and preventing "flow" in your life. By recognizing the thoughts that hold you back, you can consciously choose empowering alternatives. Awareness equals an engaged and conscious mind and is the key to becoming your greatest motivator and creator.

Actionable Step

Throughout the day, take a moment to observe your thoughts. When a negative thought arises, acknowledge it and then replace it with a positive alternative. This practice will gradually rewire your mindset for success.

3. **Visionary Power: Chart Your Epic Journey**

"You're either defined by a vision of the future or defined by the memories of the past."

—Dr. Joe Dispenza

We're all living within a vision. The question is: Are you living in your desired life vision or your default life vision?

Your vision is much more than wishful thinking. It's your roadmap to an extraordinary life. It's not just a dream—it's a powerful force that directs your energy toward your goals. It's the compass that directs your energy, creativity, and actions toward creating the future you desire.

The sad fact is that 99% of the world's population doesn't believe it can do remarkable things. So, they shoot for mediocre goals. The exciting news is that no one's future is set in stone.

By defining a clear vision, you set the stage for intentional growth and transformation. Don't let past limitations define you; instead, let your vision guide you to a blazing trail toward the new life you're meant to live.

Remember, your brain is like a muscle—learn to condition it with empowering thoughts, or it will hang out like a tormenting couch potato in your head.

Actionable Step

Explore and write down the "epic" story you aspire to "star" in. Write down a vision statement for your journey. Be bold, be specific, and let it reflect the epic life you desire. Ask yourself what sets your heart on fire and what makes you feel inspired. Big dreams attract big emotions. If you're not feeling it, start over. Let go of fear and judgment, and have fun. Revisit this vision daily to keep it at the forefront of your mind, guiding your decisions and actions.

Reflection

Have the chapters of your life been an intricate story, each page spun from the rich tales of triumph and challenges, of gained knowledge and wisdom, as mine has?

What chapters have given you light? What endings have left you broken? Like me, have you battled the dark "Knight" of the Soul wearing your cape of resilience and courage? These stages are merely the training ground, ***"The Dawning,"*** of the Epic Life Story you are here for.

A Calling

"Yes, I am a dreamer. For a dreamer is one who can only find his way by moonlight, sees the dawn before the rest of the world."

—Oscar Wilde

To you, my extraordinary soul, I offer an invitation that comes from the heart. Many of us are on the same quest—to align our deepest passions with our life's work, to liberate our creative spirits, and to thrive in the joy of doing what we love.

My invitation is simple, yet it holds the power to transform. Join me in the pursuit of your Epic Life Story. It all begins with a conversation—a gift to yourself that you may have been waiting too long to unwrap. Now is the time to put yourself first and embrace the journey of self-discovery that will lead you to the life you are meant to live.

I invite you to share your story with me, to connect through the healing power of expression, and to engage in a conversation that could be the spark of your own rebirth. Your time is now—take the first step toward the extraordinary life that awaits you to set your soul on fire.

Jane Applegath

Jane Applegath, is a trailblazer in unleashing the boundless potential within every woman. With a dynamic career as an award-winning financial advisor, television producer, certified VUCAMAX instructor, serial entrepreneur, creative scriptwriter, certified yoga instructor, and author, Jane is a master at turning vision into reality.

As the founder of the global video podcast, the Epic Vision Zone, Jane has attracted top business leaders, entrepreneurs, thought leaders, and more, inspiring women worldwide to step into their most powerful role yet—A Woman Beyond Limits.

Jane's journey is a testament to the limitless possibilities that await when you harness the genius of your mind, the magnetism of your heart, and the creative power of your imagination.

Drawing on her studies of renowned scientist and author Dr. Joe Dispenza, the VUCAMAX leadership program, and other neuroscience teachings, Jane incorporates these groundbreaking techniques into her teachings, empowering women to transcend their perceived limits.

Jane knows every woman has the potential to be a bringer of big ideas, a force of influence, and an inspiration for change. Her mission: To shatter the myths that it's too late, too hard, or too far-fetched for women to thrive and make a meaningful impact doing what they love.

Featured in Bold Journey, Voyage Phoenix, Shout Out Arizona, and numerous podcasts, Jane guides passion-driven women on a path of radical self-empowerment. She believes in more—more joy, more fulfillment, more creation—and she's here to help you unlock the EPIC VISION of your dreams and turn it into your new reality.

If you're ready to step into the life that you've always imagined, embrace your epic story, and become the heroine of your own life, Jane Applegath is your guide.

Jane Applegath
Epic Vision Zone
Scottsdale, AZ
Jane@JaneApplegath.com
JaneApplegath.com
JaneApplegath.com/contact
www.Instagram.com/JaneApplegath

Awaken Your Epic:
The Path to Becoming a Woman Beyond Limits

Step into your greatest leading role and explore what it truly means to be a limitless woman. If you are a woman who wants to liberate her past to declare her future, then this is your gateway to claiming the epic life story you are meant to live.

In an exclusive FREE 30-minute guided call, you will begin to own your voice—the most powerful force you possess to manifest who you came here to be. Join Jane Applegath for an exploratory conversation where you will connect, share, and ignite the spark that will set your soul on fire.

Don't wait. Your time is now. This is your moment to say goodbye to the supporting character you've been playing and say HELLO to YOUR EPIC STARRING ROLE.

I can't wait to meet you!

JaneApplegath.com/Book

Carla Snyder

Where Do the Dreams Begin

"Reflecting back on the tragic events of the past, it felt like this darkness would endlessly last."

—Carla J. Snyder

It was the summer of 2002. My best friend and our families gathered for the spectacle of the Mission Bay ComicCon. The melody of lapping waves created a serene contrast to the electrifying buzz resonating from the exhibition floor, where excited fans gathered to catch glimpses of movie stars and superheroes in dazzling costumes.

Amidst the vibrant chaos, my two children, Gavin, a curious 9-year-old, and Jonna, a spirited 12-year-old, reveled in the magic of the moment. Little did I know this day would etch itself into the chronicles of my life, altering its trajectory forever.

Suddenly, in a cosmic play of irony, the universe literally brought me to my knees as I collapsed to the ground.

I remember the surrounding laughter fading, replaced by the palpable beating of my heart. Vulnerability and panic suspended time, as fear siphoned every ounce of my self-reliance down to my bones. My mind screamed, "I'm a single parent with two young children. This can't be happening!"

In an instant, my world had tilted off its axis. I swallowed back the fear of revelation, and uttered to my friend's husband, "Don, I can't get up."

Uncertainty and hope collide on a day where the tapestry of ComicCon's fantastical tales became the backdrop for an unexpected chapter in my own story—a chapter that would propel me into a journey of self-discovery, transformation, and the profound realization that sometimes the most extraordinary narratives unfold within the confines of our own lives.

Flashback

"Experience gives us the test first, the lessons later."

—Naomi Judd

Many of us go through our days believing tomorrow is a guarantee. The years fly by and before we know it, we're suddenly jolted by the urgency of our reality, asking what's my life all about?

I thought back to when I was eighteen, orchestrating phone banks and registration walks for a politician. That was the moment my desire to lead others seeded itself in my young heart and soul.

I had found my passion. However, my journey had only just begun.

College became a playground for my ambitions. I delved into co-creating a transformative opportunity for freshmen, channeling their energies into community-based experiences to foster engagement and retention. By the time I received my bachelor's degree, I had woven a diverse tapestry of experiences.

*Experiences, I have learned, are our building blocks. They are not random occurrences, but deliberate challenges, hurdles, and trials orchestrated to strengthen us for the journey ahead.

When the corporate world beckoned, I eagerly embraced the challenge of developing a nationwide lecture series and embarked on a cross-country expedition to educate practitioners. However, my success was short-lived. After a few years, my position was eliminated.

*I heard a voice inside me say, "Listen to your desires and courageously follow where they lead. Each challenging moment is shaping you, making you stronger, wiser, and more resilient."

Losing that job became the cosmic nudge into my inaugural entrepreneurial pursuit. I began working for a soft skills training company. I quickly learned that I had taken a leap into the deep end of a billion-dollar industry—the leadership development space—where I struggled to stay afloat amidst the turbulent waves of unchartered waters.

*Over the years I have come to understand the significance of trust—trusting in the process, trusting that everything happens for a reason, and trusting that reason is there to assist me.

In the absence of mentorship or guidance, the uphill battle continued until fate intervened, and my fortunes changed upon transitioning to the Arizona marketplace. This became the launching pad for a high-level business development role, where I built a thriving territory, surpassing $10 million in sales.

*Today I understand the profound value of giving back. I understand that the more we give, the more we receive.

"For it is when we give of ourselves that we truly give."

—Kahlil Gibran

Building relationships beyond the transactional became my business foundation. A pivotal moment unfolded when one of my customers introduced me to the American Society of Training and Development. This connection proved instrumental in expanding my business horizons. It was here that I discovered the profound impact of giving back, a value I hold dear to this day.

Taking a leadership role, I contributed to designing monthly education programs, a gratifying experience that further enriched my journey. However, setbacks weren't far behind, each disguised in different costumes that tested my resilience.

*Throughout my life I have sought to guide others. However, experience has taught me that to walk through the maze of life, we all need the light of wisdom and the guidance of goodness. And we need to

learn when to turn to others for support and assistance, rather than allow pride to be our downfall.

Setbacks seem to come in waves. The recession hit and an acquisition takeover of the firm I worked for transpired. Then a respected customer challenge tested my confidence. It was during this time that the latter incident prompted me to seek guidance from another longtime customer. This call for help proved to be a transformative step along my journey, providing insights that fueled my growth.

That Pivotal Day

> *"An inner voice is growing, calling me to task, the revelation that it's time to remove the mask."*
>
> —Carla J. Snyder

And so, the threads of my past experiences converged on that pivotal day in San Diego, a day bathed in the warmth of summer, surrounded by family, and immersed in the excitement of ComicCon. My children, Gavin, and Jonna, added an extra layer of joy to the occasion. Little did I know that this day would etch itself into the narrative of my life in ways I could never have anticipated.

As I found myself on the ground, uttering those life-altering words to Don, my best friend's husband, the echoes of my life's journey reverberated. The collision of vulnerability and strength encapsulated the essence of a lifetime filled with triumphs, challenges, and unwavering dedication to service.

In an instant, the trajectory of my life had taken a monumental turn that would ultimately lead me to discover my life's divine purpose—my North Star.

Lingering pain and the development of a limp led me to the door of the orthopedic surgeon. This was the unexpected stage that shook the foundations of my life—a pivotal moment that demanded change and foresaw the consequences of maintaining the status quo.

I recall my hands shaking as the door swung open revealing the doctor holding a 3x5 piece of paper with a name on it—a harbinger of the words that would alter the course of my journey. I held the surgeon's gaze as I listened to words that cut through me like a knife.

"Don't let anyone convince you to get your hips replaced, which you will need to do, but first, you need major, potentially life-changing surgery to rebuild your back."

Time suddenly stood still. Fear clutched at my heart like a vise as the gravity of the situation hit me. My life was abruptly fraught with challenges that could redefine everything. The prospect of physical, and potentially life-changing surgery sent an earthquake through my consciousness.

I stood at a crossroads, and the choice before me carried profound implications.

My North Star

> *"Be the cliff against which the waves continually break;*
> *but it stands firm and tames the fury of the water around it."*

—Marcus Aurelius

Just as explorers rely on the North Star as their symbol of guidance and direction, aiding them to navigate the seas, our North Star is what inspires and influences us. It's the fundamental ethos of our divine, purposeful life, and the ultimate realization of our happiness.

Over the next several months, what unfolded became a testament to unwavering faith and an unyielding resolve. Fueled by a crystallized vision of Tina Turner's electrifying performances, I was determined to re-discover my North Star; to dance again, to reclaim the joy and freedom of movement.

My new journey became a tapestry woven with the threads of resilience and the unwavering belief that this turning point was not an end but a beginning. Each therapy session, each moment of excruciating pain became a step towards the envisioned future—a future where the pain of the fall would be overshadowed by the triumph of overcoming it.

Over the next eight years, I sculpted my North Star—the guiding light that urged me to uplevel my game.

As the journey unfolded, I held onto the vision of dancing like Tina Turner, a vision that empowered me to navigate the uncertain waters with courage and conviction. This was not just a physical recovery but a celebration of resilience and the unwavering spirit within.

This was a time when the decision to embark on a transformative journey was made, setting the stage for a chapter of healing, growth, and the triumphant return to the dance of life.

In the Groove

> *"An inner voice is growing, calling me to task.*
> *The revelation that it's time to remove the mask."*

—Unknown

Many people, in my experience, don't take the time to consider what sets their hearts on fire, what brings joy to their lives, and what fuels them. Day after day, week after week, and year after year, we move through life on automatic pilot, without much thought of what we once dreamed about.

*But wisdom has taught me that we are here for so much more. We are here not just to survive, but to thrive, and that comes by stepping into our true calling in life—our North Star.

It's a calling that beckons us to "Get in the Groove"…. of our life.

As fate would have it, destiny led me to the booth of Grand Canyon University (GCU). The representative, sensing a dream deferred, posed a game-changing question: "Ever considered getting a master's degree?" Twelve days later, I found myself in my first class, navigating a realm where potential met opportunity.

The initial moments were filled with butterflies. As I embarked on this educational odyssey, the GCU dashboard displayed a beacon of solace—the "Prayer Request" button, summoned frequently during those early classes. In 18 months, adorned with straight A's, I not only completed the program but ascended into the hallowed space of the honors society.

My professional journey took a synchronized leap, where I immersed myself in the intricacies of career transition. Resume writing, interviewing techniques, negotiating strategies, and onboarding intricacies became the threads I wove into my skill set.

Armed with a Master of Science in Leadership, I received a beckoning call to teach management and supervisory training at the community college—an opportunity that would hone my leadership skills further.

This was a chapter of growth and learning, of resilience and perseverance that broke the shackles of my comfort zones to reach new pinnacles. I forged meaningful connections in business, education, and non-profit leadership. It was a time when dreams collided with reality, challenges were transformed into stepping stones, and the pursuit of knowledge became a bridge to new opportunities.

*I had learned to stand strong and tame the turbulent waters around me.

I had gained the strength, the experience, and the wisdom to step bravely into yet another chapter of my life. I transitioned from the for-profit sector to the nonprofit arena. The shift came at a considerable cost, requiring me to start lower on the economic food chain.

Armed with communication, sales, and teaching acumen, I deployed my skills to impact lives—both the dedicated staff and the grateful recipients of our services. The transition marked a profound shift towards a life of servant leadership, a calling that resonated deeply with my essence.

*You know you've reached a pivotal turning point in your journey when the work you do aligns with your heart."

The Best Is Yet to Come

> *"Life has a funny way of putting us through the dark to show us the light. For without the darkness there is no light. All the setbacks, obstacles, and challenges are mere steppingstones calling us to brave the journey to our greater destination."*
>
> —Carla J. Snyder

The chapters of my varied career have imparted rich wisdom, intuition, and extraordinary guidance skills. These are the fabric of my quintessential coaching and leadership toolkit.

The setbacks, the lessons, and the shifts have each contributed to the person I am today.

*Know that you cannot change what happens to you, but you can always change how you react to it.

What encapsulates the essence of your journey? What early struggles and transformative moments have you experienced?

Have you donned a cloak woven with threads of personal resilience, faith, and courage as I have? These are testaments to the transformative power of our experiences.

These are the narratives of growth that become invaluable wisdom gained through the trials and tribulations of defining your North Star and recasting a career with purpose.

Reflecting on the growth and evolution spurred by my journey, I know we are built to do so much more than simply survive by making a living.

One of the joys of my work today is helping clients find their true calling—their North Star—so that they can boldly thrive doing work they love. When you are living with purpose, it's much easier to weather the storms and become the cliff on which the waves break.

Here are three Purpose-Powered Pillars for Crafting a Career You Love:

Pillar 1: Knowing When to Hold Them

(Navigate with Confidence)

Embedded in the fabric of my journey is the wisdom to stick with a career or educational path with patience and consistent effort, especially when an innate sense tells you that this path aligns with your core values and passion. This resilience, akin to holding onto a winning hand, has been a cornerstone of my success. It's a belief rooted in the core understanding that enduring challenges with unwavering commitment often leads to profound growth and fulfillment.

Pillar 2: Knowing When to Fold Them

(The Art of Self-Awareness)

Equally crucial is the ability to be painfully honest with oneself. It involves recognizing when it's time to walk away, whether from a personal or professional endeavor. This is the art of self-awareness. The metaphorical folding of one's cards signifies the courage to let go of what no longer serves you, making room for new opportunities and growth. This belief underscores the importance of acknowledging when a chapter needs closure for a fresh narrative to unfold.

Pillar 3: Knowing How to Engage the Best Mentor/Guide

(Align with Success)

The journey is dynamic, and so is the need for guidance. The third pillar centers on the art of engaging the right mentor or guide, recognizing that this entity evolves as you progress through your journey. Whether it's seeking advice, learning from someone's experiences, or gaining insights for the next step, aligning with the right mentor becomes a compass guiding you toward your desired destination.

These three Pillars nurtured and refined my own transformative career journey. They served as beacons for navigating a path forward. They encapsulate the essence of resilience, honesty, and strategic guidance—tools that not only shaped my growth but have proven invaluable to the countless individuals I've led through their own transformations.

As I stand at the intersection of my past and present, the journey unfolds like the turning pages of a well-worn book. In this moment, my vision is clear, fueled by a passion to guide others through the labyrinth of self-discovery and professional alignment, steering them toward their North Star.

It's a vision born from the struggles I once faced—the search for that elusive intersection where passion seamlessly meets the perfect professional position. The desire to wake up every day feeling that work is a joyous expression of one's purpose.

Artistic Expression

> *"We are all born creators. Art is the tangible expression of creative energy. Creativity is your life force energy flowing through you."*
>
> —Adam Roa

Does your vision intertwine with the pull of liberating your artistic expression, as mine does?

At our core we are all creators, whether that means organizing your closet, preparing a family meal, doing your taxes, or deciding what to wear…or using it as an expression of your life story, as I have throughout this narrative.

Creative expression is a healing force I discovered when I penned my first book of poetry. The creative inner voice, once buried beneath the weight of uncertainty, found a harmonious melody in the words I crafted

Through the Carla J. Snyder 24-hour rule, I've learned to navigate challenging, emotion-filled situations by turning inward and engaging in artistic pursuits—whether it's poetry, journaling, painting, or other forms. This practice has proven to be a transformative tool, a key to resolving delicate situations with grace and success.

An Invitation

I extend an invitation—a call to action. I see so many grappling with the same quest to align passion with profession, to liberate their creative inner voices and thrive doing work they love.

My ask is simple yet profound: join me in the adventure of seeking your North Star. It begins with a conversation, a gift to yourself that might have been postponed for too long. The time has come to put yourself first, to embark on the transformative journey of self-discovery.

I invite you to relate your experiences to mine, to discover the healing power of artistic expression, and to engage in a conversation that could be the catalyst for your own transformative journey.

Your *IMPACT TRANSFORMATION* awaits.

Seize it!

Carla Snyder

A consummate leader both in the community and on the national stage, Carla J. Snyder has received numerous accolades, including the Her Story award from the Global Women's Peace Network in May 2024 and the Phoenix Business Journal's Outstanding Woman in Business Award in March 2024 for her contributions to both the non-profit and corporate arenas. In 2021, she was honored as the International Woman of the Year for Promoting Peace.

As a published poet with her work "Liberte" and co-producer of the documentary "Climate of Hope: Cities Saving the World," Carla combines creativity and advocacy to inspire and educate. Her expertise as a career coach has guided individuals from new college graduates to C-Suite executives, helping them discover and achieve their personal and professional North Stars, where their passions align with purposeful positions.

As a keynote speaker and workshop facilitator, she provides invaluable tips, techniques, and inspiration to navigate the ever-changing world of work and manage transitions throughout a lifetime. With a focus on collaborating with C-Suite leaders across various industries, she addresses business's most pressing challenges and creates sustainable solutions.

Certified as a leadership and sales skills trainer, Carla has worked with both corporations and non-profits to enhance employee productivity and morale. Raising two children as a single mom, she earned her Master of Science in Leadership from Grand Canyon University.

Featured in the Desert Ridge Publication for her ongoing impact and dedication to making a difference, Carla J. Snyder continues to inspire, lead, and transform lives, helping others find their path to purpose and fulfillment.

Carla Snyder
Impact Transformation, LLC
Scottsdale, AZ
602-400-0502
Carla@CarlaJSnyder.com
https://CarlaJSnyder.com

Discover Your North Star:
Free 15-Minute Career Breakthrough Call

Unlock the secrets to a fulfilling career with our Discover Your North Star 15-Minute Free Career Breakthrough Call. Whether you are a new graduate or a seasoned executive, this consultation is designed to help you uncover your true passions, values, and purpose. Transform your professional life and align your career with your core beliefs and aspirations. Book your free call now and take the first step toward a more empowered and purposeful future.

https://CarlaJSnyder.com

Sue Mandell

Deserving Second Chances

"Don't think there are no second chances.
Life always offers you a SECOND CHANCE...
It's called TOMORROW."

—Nicholas Sparks, American novelist and screenwriter

I'm one who has lived the lowest of the lows, and by God's grace, I climbed out of the gutter to become a contributing member of society. The question becomes: Do people like me deserve a second chance? Why would someone, anyone, bother to give me a second chance? Why would I even want to go through that process? My life had no structure to it. Becoming responsible, starting all over again, why? Second chances are reserved for people who've never known the struggle, the uphill battle of every step. So said my keen intellect.

A new chapter in the story of life was unfolding. New chances offer redemption, growth, and renewal. They are a turning point where mistakes and setbacks are not the end of the road. They're only what you can see until you turn the next corner. As I turned that corner, I had to make a choice. Will the rest of my life be more of the same? More incomprehensible demoralization? Or was I finally desperate enough to look for my second chance?

The Turmoil of Youth

At 29, life was a non-stop party. As a bartender in a bustling Navy town, I thrived on the nightly excitement and the constant attention from sailors. I was having the time of my life—until I wasn't.

Like every other morning, he came walking downstairs. However, unlike any other morning, he was looking at us, his wife and I, sitting at the kitchen table. I could see his eyes as he was taking a look down at his watch, then he was looking back at us. Shaking his head with such a glare of disgust and contempt, he turned and began slowly walking back upstairs. We'd been up all night, and for me, I was up all night, *again*.

For the first time, I felt a crushing wave of shame and remorse. As I saw my friend's husband's disgusted look, it hit me like never before. His normal life contrasted starkly with my chaotic existence, marked by a haze of drugs and alcohol. In that moment, I saw myself through his eyes—a realization that devastated and awakened me. That look of contempt on his face was palpable and devastating. My best friend's husband saw me for exactly what I was, a drug addicted alcoholic.

I don't know where they came from, since my brain had never even formed the thought, but the words came tumbling out of my mouth as if a dam had burst. *I have a problem*, and *I don't know what to do about it*. I was horrified.

Looking back over my decades of sobriety, I could easily say that those years were effortless but that would be far from the truth. If I said anything even close to that, it would be one of the biggest whoppers I've ever told; and I've told some doozies.

According to Forbes, *the biggest whopper ever told is an idea that people will accept a lie as a fact, if it's told long enough and loud enough.* Remember when the world was flat? Universal truths, like the world being flat, would be considered a whopper today if told as factual, which science has obviously proven false.

It was the perfect storm, and I was desperate enough, thankfully. Today, I get to do my best to live life one day at a time. At times it's one hour, or one minute, or one second at a time. Every now and then, it's even one breath at a time. My big audacious goal in life is striving for progress, not perfection.

People Like Me

Living in Seattle, WA, I had to learn to walk around the alcoholics in Pioneer Square. They were either passed out or drinking *something* from a brown paper bag. **They Were Disgusting**. They were dirty and smelly, and their clothes looked like rags from my cleaning supplies box. I don't think they had too many teeth left in their mouths, either. Now, *that's* what an alcoholic looks like, not me. Little did I know.

Somewhere along the line, as I was growing up, I learned that people like me—people struggling with alcoholism, and addiction and falling so far down the ladder of respectability—weren't destined for success. The societal expectation was that I would end up nowhere. However, I dared to challenge that limiting belief. People *like me* aren't supposed to live happy, productive, and fulfilling lives. People like me are supposed to die in the streets. If they are alone when it happens, they aren't found for days. I was terrified. Terrified that if I went back to drinking, I wouldn't be able to stop again. I wouldn't be able to stop again, and I wouldn't be lucky enough to die next time. I had no doubts I would end up like the alcoholics who didn't die from their disease. I knew I would end up in jails or institutions.

But not me! That's not my story. Mine is one of second chances. By God's grace, I've been able to show up for my loved ones. I've stayed sober through the most difficult times and been there when they needed me most.

For as long as I can remember, my mom was my best friend, and I was her little Susie. I didn't know how rare that was to be an alcoholic woman and have a close relationship with my mom. I was only two years sober when she got *the diagnosis*. People like me don't know how to show up when it's especially tough. Then *people like me* miss saying goodbye to loved ones. It's just too hard to be a responsible grownup.

Mom was so afraid. She was afraid of dying, afraid of leaving us, and afraid of what would happen to my dad. Dad was paralyzed on his entire right side from a stroke 15 years earlier. She was terrified that without her there to help, Dad wouldn't be able to get to his doctor's appointments or do his laundry. How was he going to get groceries or cook meals? Was he going to be OK? What if he got sick? Would he survive and be able to get around without her help?

My mother's greatest gift to me was allowing me to be her trusted confidant. Mom was able to confide those fears in me, being honest about what she was going through. She couldn't talk like that with Dad; he was already devastated knowing that he was going to lose his life partner after so many decades. A few months after that first confidential conversation with my mom, my best friend passed away.

Eight years later, my dad had been so independent that he bought and wore out *three* electric scooters. He volunteered at the local high school and rode his scooter five miles roundtrip to tutor students in English as a second language, even when it was raining. That round trip took him at least an hour. I never knew about his volunteering. I learned about this from a newspaper article at the bottom of his nightstand.

I eventually became my father's caregiver. Dad and I would sit together for hours, listening to books on tape. He loved playing blackjack, and he taught us all to count cards when I was very young. During this season of our life together, I would load him up in the car with a packed suitcase hidden in the trunk. Telling him we were going out to grab a bite to eat, he'd eventually catch on to where we were going. As I hit the road between my house and the casinos, we were making many happy memories, which I get to replay in my mind's eye, as often as I choose.

I also got my passion for baseball and the San Francisco Giants from Dad. We watched the games together all during the season. As we watched the Giants in a playoff game, I held Dad's hand as he let out his final breath. People like me don't show up when it's tough, *but I got to*. You may have guessed by now that family has become most important to me in sobriety.

For Over 60 Years

My entire life was marked by tension with my brother, unable to spend more than two hours together without conflict. Yet, understanding him through the lens of our distinct personalities transformed our relationship. Our conversations are now more about connection rather than correction. It isn't that I didn't love him for all those years because I did. He's my brother, so of course I love him. It's just that I didn't like him very much. Everything is always a debate, and he's the expert.

My brother is incredibly intelligent, the smartest person I knew growing up, and he continually corrected me. Trust me when I say he has no problem letting me know just how smart he is. He must have the last word; he was condescending and patronizing. Me? It left me feeling incompetent, incapable, and inadequate.

Every time I opened my mouth, we fought about *something*. I'm sure he didn't like me. If he did, he wouldn't always be picking fights with me. My brother even got into a huge fight with my dad one time. He knew all the science, so he insisted that parallel lines would eventually meet in infinity. My brother absolutely cannot be wrong. He blames it on his high intelligence. However, it's his personality that won't allow it. He must always be the smartest person in the room. I learned that this is in his DNA.

Nothing Has Meaning

Nothing has meaning, but the meaning I give it. This has become a universal truth for me. It's such a simple idea, and it took a long time for me to *get it*. I began understanding that all those antagonistic things he would say to me, those arguments, and a lifetime of thinking his behavior and actions toward me were all about me. By understanding the power of the system and its tools, I learned his behavior was all about him. He didn't say those things to hurt me on purpose. It's in his DNA.

I was learning about a methodology to increase sales exponentially. That's when I learned of the power of personalities. Prior to understanding the four personalities, I was left feeling helpless, hopeless, and powerless. What I've learned is that life changes, and it's all about values. His intellect, combined with his personality, influences him so that he *cannot* be wrong. It wouldn't matter who he was talking to. His need to be right is as strong and unconscious as his need for air.

I spent 60 years saying everything I could think of to make him understand *me*. If I could get him to just stop talking and listen for a minute. Life would be so much easier, if he would stop correcting me and answering questions I didn't ask.

Then a miracle happened! I stopped. I just stopped. I stopped talking until I was blue in the face. I stopped expecting him to understand *me*. I began understanding *him*, learning what's important and what's not important to him.

We have happier and less contentious conversations every day. I talk to my brother the way he wants, directly and to the point. He doesn't like long-winded questions or statements. He just wants data and no chit-chat, so I do my best to be succinct and to the point and use fewer words than I'm used to. I do my best to use words that light up *his* neural network. It's like hitting a high score on a video game or the finale of fireworks on the 4th of July. When he needs the last word or feels the need to correct me, I get it and no longer take it personally. None of these things have anything to do with me. It's part of his personality and in his DNA. *It's not personal, it's personality!*

We decided to build a home together, and we now live under the same roof. By leveraging the communication tools and techniques, I felt a major shift in my deepest feelings. This could never have happened before. Sadly, just a few short weeks after moving in, he fell and broke his ankle. I've been his caregiver and chauffeur for a year. Remember, *people like me* are not supposed to be able to show up when it's tough. The greatest miracle of all, is that I *want* to help when he needs me, and he said *I love you* without prompting. I can probably count the number of times he said I love you and always after I had said it. Then, a while ago, as he was dropping me off at the airport, and as I was getting out of the car, he said, "Have a safe trip; I love you."

Today, my life is full of miracles, and I am blessed. I've not had a drink in decades. However, I get to help my brother when he needs me. I've had two extremely successful careers, and I've retired and started a business. *People like me* do deserve second chances.

Exercise

1. **Who are three people in your life that you want a healthier relationship with? (This could be a family member, friend, or a business relationship.)**

   _____

   _____

   _____

2. **What are two values you believe are important to each of those individuals? How can you honor those values?**

   _____

   _____

   _____

   _____

3. **How is your personality different from these people? How are they similar?**

   _____

   _____

   _____

   _____

The Challenge

I urge you to shift your perspective: seek first to understand others' unique viewpoints and personalities. By embracing this approach, you can transform your relationships and foster deeper connections. Make this *your* big audacious goal; make the people in your world matter. Let them know how important they are and do it in ways that are important to them. Light up their neural networks like the 4th of July. Hint: you can do this by learning what's important to them and why.

Things To Remember

Communication is about the message. It's about the message you wish to transmit and the message that's received. You want those messages to be identical. However, too often they're not. That's because everyone has their own unique life experiences and backgrounds. What those experiences mean to us: those are our *filters*. Because of these filters, we hear the same words and messages differently. It is also known as miscommunication.

For as long as I can remember, I've been taught to speak to others the way I want to be spoken to and to treat them how I want to be treated. The Golden Rule works if the person across from you is just like you. Your personalities are a match. The Platinum Rule, now that's different. The Platinum Rule allows you to treat people the way *they* want to be treated and to speak the way *they* want to be spoken to.

Everything In Life Is A Choice

Based on my story, how long will you let your relationships suffer because you speak different languages? Great relationships are built on great communication.

Everything in life is about *choice*. The decisions we make or don't make, the actions we take or don't take are all choices. If you decide not to make any changes, nothing will change. You get to choose how you want to communicate with the people in your world: your loved ones, friends, coworkers, employees, and employers. Unless you are in a cave alone in the world, you must communicate, so why not learn to do it effectively?

I invite you to join me in exploring how to deepen relationships that are important to you and even salvage some you've given up on. How can better communication ever be anything but a good thing? Better connection makes happier lives, happier relationships, and happier tomorrows.

Learning about the four primary personalities of the world and understanding why someone makes the decisions they make has only changed everything for me. I have a friendship with my brother that wasn't possible before. By using this unparalleled communication tool in K-12 schools, no child will have to wonder if they matter. I wanted to make more money and have an impact. What I got was so much greater. People like me don't get to have such heartfelt memories. But I do.

Sue Mandell

Author | MAOM | KBNA | Licensed & Certified Communications Expert | Master Practitioner NLP

As an international best-selling author and a woman who has shared stages with Martha Stewart, Suzanne Somers, and Les Brown, Sue Mandell is who you want to show you a simple step-by-step system to becoming an ACE Speaker; how to grab their attention and have fun while speaking.

As an Award-Winning Speaker, she has spoken at Carnegie Hall, The Harvard Club of Boston, and The NY Bar Association. She has been honored as the "Woman of the Year" by a national non-profit and has been interviewed by major news networks, such as ABC, CBS, NBC, and radio stations across the country.

Sue has her master's degree in business, is a licensed personality communications expert, and is an NLP master practitioner. She's been assisting others to permanently change undesired behaviors and overcome limiting beliefs and addictive behaviors for more than four decades. Sue has done this while helping her clients to increase their sales exponentially and drastically improve every relationship in their lives.

Sue Mandell
Sue Mandell, Inc.
Goodyear, AZ
Sue@ChooseYourHabits.com
ChooseYourHabits.com

10 Tips for Communication Mastery
Personally—Sales—Business

Download these 10 Communication Mastery Tips for some immediate benefits:

- Improved Relationships: Learn how to build stronger connections with family, friends, and colleagues through clear and compassionate communication.

- Conflict Resolution Skills: Discover how to handle disagreements effectively and turn tense situations into opportunities for understanding

- Confidence Boost: Gain the tools to express your thoughts and feelings assertively, without fear of misunderstanding or rejection.

- Enhanced Listening: Master the art of active listening to make others feel heard, valued, and respected.

- Clarity in Expression: Develop the ability to convey your ideas and emotions with precision, reducing confusion and miscommunication.

- Empathy Building: Learn techniques to better understand and respond to the emotions and needs of others.

- Workplace Success: Improve professional interactions, from managing difficult conversations to building rapport with colleagues.

- Stronger Family Bonds: Overcome communication barriers that may strain relationships at home, creating a more harmonious environment.

- Stress Reduction: Minimize the anxiety and frustration that often accompany miscommunication or unresolved issues.

- Empowerment in Recovery: Align your communication skills with your personal growth journey, reinforcing your progress in recovery and personal development.

These tips are a practical, actionable resource designed to create immediate positive change in how you interact with others as you strive for more meaningful connections.

https://bit.ly/3CaJKrA

Dr. Vasundhara (Vasu) Tolia
Art of Reinvention: A Journey from Healing Patients to Healing Minds

A Shattered Dream

The acrid scent of antiseptic hung in the air, mingling with the soft hum of monitors while I peeked at the lining of the intestines. When I would finish the endoscopy, I would go out, explain the findings, further the management plan, and alleviate the parents' anxiety, until they lightened up. For decades, this had been my world—a realm where precise and life-altering decisions were routine. I, Dr. Vasundhara (called Vasu) Tolia, stood at the pinnacle of my career as a pediatric gastroenterologist until everything changed.

With the arrival of a new department chairman, the career I had painstakingly built over 35 years began to unravel quickly. The multifaceted role I cherished—clinician, researcher, teacher, mentor—was slipping through my fingers. I was told to focus only on basic research. Academic politics, a force I had naively underestimated, was threatening to reshape my entire professional identity.

I discussed the changes of being asked to do basic research only with my husband. He felt that there must be more than was obvious and he was right. I faced a phase in my workplace that I had never anticipated.

What I didn't know then was that this crisis would ignite a transformation journey, leading me from the structured world of medicine to the liberating realm of art.

The end of one dream sometimes paves the way for another, waiting to be discovered.

The Unplanned Path

To understand how I arrived at this turning point, I must journey back to the bustling streets of Kolkata, India, in the 1950s and 1960s. I was the third child in a family with three brothers, born into a society steeped in tradition, yet energized by the spirit of a newly independent nation. My parents were from the state of Gujarat. They had migrated there in search of a better life. Kolkata was a city where old-world norms often stifled modern aspirations, particularly for girls. While my brothers had all the freedom, I was sheltered. My life centered around education. My parents, determined to provide us with the best foundation, poured their hearts into our academic studies, a gift for which I remain eternally grateful.

However, the conservative nature of our society limited my experiences, particularly with activities like sports and outdoor adventures, which were then considered 'inappropriate' for girls . Even riding a bicycle was off-limits for most girls. A prediction from an astrologer instilled a deep-seated family fear of water, preventing me from ever learning to swim also.

A childhood encounter with a stray dog also left me with a lasting fear of animals.

These limitations could have defined me. However, they instead fueled a desire to learn, grow, and push against the boundaries imposed on me. My parents' unwavering commitment to our education laid a solid foundation for what was to come, even if it meant sacrificing some of the carefree aspects of childhood.

In the ninth grade, I faced a choice that would set the course of my life. I was ready to pursue arts, with no inkling that medicine was in my future. I had no role models in the medical field and no burning desire to heal the sick. However, fate, as they say, had other plans. My best friend had an older brother who was studying medicine. On her encouragement, I chose science.

Just like that, I became what I now jokingly call "an accidental doctor." Here's the thing about accidents—sometimes they lead you exactly where you're meant to be.

Once I embarked on this trail, I threw myself into it with everything I had. That's just how I am. This unexpected decision would shape my entire life, leading me down a path I never imagined. However, it would ultimately fulfill me in ways I couldn't have foreseen.

Love Amid Chaos

My journey through medical school was far from smooth sailing. As I began my studies, political unrest gripped West Bengal. The tumultuous Naxalite movement disrupted our lives, throwing the entire education system into chaos. After two smooth years, repeated exam postponements extended my five-year medical program to a frustrating seven and a half years. Those extra years were filled with uncertainty, fear, and a sense of lost time. The world around me was in turmoil. I felt as though my dreams were slipping away.

There were immense challenges during those years. The constant disruptions, the long waits between exams, and the ongoing political instability created an environment of extreme stress and unpredictability. There was little room for peace or productivity in the conventional sense. These years instead became a test of endurance and commitment to my chosen path.

Those years in medical school, despite their challenges, or perhaps because of them, shaped me greatly. They instilled in me a deep appreciation for education, resilience in the face of adversity, and a determination to make the most of every opportunity. Little did I know then how well these qualities would serve me in the unexpected turns my life would take in the years to come.

Amidst the mayhem, I found a silver lining. I met my future husband in college. We connected instantly, and as the saying goes, the rest is history. Our bond, forged in the crucible of those challenging times, grew stronger daily.

We supported each other through the uncertainties, the long waits between the exams, and the constant fear of further disruptions. We married just before leaving for the United States for further studies, embarking on a wonderful journey that has now spanned almost five decades.

Looking back, I see that the adversities we faced during those early years not only tested our resilience but also laid the foundation for a lifelong partnership built on mutual support and understanding.

New Beginnings, New Battles

Moving to the United States marked the beginning of a new chapter, with its own challenges. I was a young doctor in a foreign land, navigating an unfamiliar healthcare system and cultural landscape. However, the tenacity I had cultivated during my turbulent years in Kolkata served me well.

I decided to specialize in Pediatrics, while my husband chose internal medicine. The grueling schedule during the three years of training—exhausting overnight calls and 36-hour shifts—tested my endurance. There were moments of self-doubt, homesickness, and sheer fatigue. I persevered.

Towards the end of my residency, we were blessed with identical twin sons. Raising two infants while balancing a demanding career was no small feat. However, I embraced it wholeheartedly. My mother's frequent visits were a blessing, providing much-needed support. Her presence also helped us to instill our cultural values in my sons.

I was determined to give my children opportunities that I never had. They participated in sports, music, and various activities that nurtured their talents. We spoke Gujarati at home, celebrated both American and Indian holidays, and told them stories from our mythology. Regular trips to India kept them connected to their roots.

Throughout this journey, my husband's unwavering support was my cornerstone. Together, we built a home blending two cultures—a sanctuary where dreams were nurtured and values were passed down.

Rising to the Top

When I was about to graduate as a pediatrician, I was exposed to the emerging sub-specialty of pediatric gastroenterology. It fascinated me. The first pediatric gastroenterologist in Michigan had just joined our hospital. I seized the opportunity to train under him, aiming to become the second specialist in this field in our state.

However, my fellowship was far from straightforward. During my training, I realized that to become fully qualified, I needed to learn flexible endoscopy - a skill my current teacher had never learned. Undeterred, I ventured into local adult GI programs to learn these essential procedures. This initiative led to a significant milestone: I became the first person to perform a flexible endoscopy on a child at my institution, establishing our pediatric endoscopy unit in the state.

This experience taught me another valuable lesson: sometimes, to advance in your field, you need to seek knowledge beyond your immediate environment. It also instilled in me a deep appreciation for practical skills as well as theoretical knowledge. As I settled into my career by joining the attending staff at the same hospital, I felt a void, Something was missing. I didn't have a mentor to guide me through the complexities of academia. This became glaringly apparent when I attended my first national meeting in my specialty. I had nothing to present and no project to pursue. It was a bleak realization.

Determined not to let this setback define me, I promised myself: "I will be my own mentor." This mantra still guides me today. I started small, with case reports and retrospective studies on unusual findings. However, my hunger for knowledge and growth led me to seek colleagues who could help me develop prospective randomized trials. Slowly but surely, my work began to gain recognition.

I'll never forget the thrill of presenting my first major conference paper. Standing before my peers and sharing my findings, I felt a profound sense of belonging and accomplishment. It validated my hard work and reassured me that I was on the right track. I was soon presenting multiple papers at every meeting. My abstracts were evolving into full manuscripts published in peer-reviewed journals.

My journey up the academic ladder wasn't easy. Achieving tenure was a grueling process. However, I persisted. Eventually, I became a full-tenured professor and division director at my institution. I was invited to join editorial boards, write editorials, and even started a fellowship program to train the next generation of pediatric gastroenterologists.

Looking back, I realize that my early experiences in establishing the endoscopy unit and learning new skills had prepared me for this role. I was able to impart not just knowledge but also the importance of initiative, adaptability with colleagues, and learning to do multidisciplinary projects with my trainees. I was living my dream—making a difference in the lives of sick children, advancing medical knowledge, and nurturing young doctors. My husband often remarked that just hearing about the sheer number of tasks I juggled was exhausting. However, it was second nature for me. When I committed to something, I gave it my all. I had overcome numerous challenges, breaking new ground in my field, and was nearing the zenith of my career.

Life was good… until it wasn't.

The Roadblock

At this glorious juncture of my career, institutional politics and conflicting interests were reshaping the landscape of my department. My years of dedication and achievements held less weight in the face of their new priorities. The realization was bitter. It opened my eyes to the harsh realities of academia that I had somehow managed to avoid for so long.

Faced with an impossible choice—uproot our life and my husband's thriving career for me to continue in academia elsewhere or step away from the academic dreams I had built over three and a half decades—I chose stability for my family. I decided to transition into private practice, staying local, figuring that adding a few more papers to my over 150 publications wasn't going to define my legacy differently.

The decision was heart-wrenching. It felt like I was being forced to abandon a significant part of my identity. As I grappled with this new reality, a small voice inside me whispered of new possibilities and unexplored paths waiting to be discovered.

Little did I know that this roadblock, painful as it was, would divert my life to an entirely new field of action—one that would ultimately be more fulfilling than I could have ever imagined. Sometimes, what seems like an ending is merely the beginning of a new chapter. The canvas of life was ready for a fresh stroke of paint.

A Blank Canvas

The decision to choose security for my family life made me start a private practice, staying local. The transition was anything but smooth. While I was able to do some research due to my reputation, it just wasn't fulfilling enough. A growing restlessness that I couldn't shake began to bother me. Instead of continuing as a frustrated physician, I started to explore alternatives. The thought of retirement loomed large, accompanied by a relentless fear. How could I transition from a life filled with purpose to one of complete void?

That's when I decided to explore the world of art. I began with music, taking harmonium lessons and dabbling in singing and karaoke. When that proved challenging due to inconsistent teacher availability, I turned to visual art, enrolling in basic lessons to learn the fundamentals.

Those early days were incredibly frustrating. I was a novice, struggling with brushes and paints, unable to grasp concepts like light, shadow, values, and tones. Determining the best medium to work in was a dilemma. My initial works were mere copies of photos, lacking originality.

In a few years, I pushed myself out of my comfort zone again. I began experimenting, moving away from representational art and toward semi-abstract and abstract forms. This transition was both liberating and terrifying. Some days, I almost gave up, questioning whether I should even bother to learn something so different. However, it changed slowly. I started to see the interplay of light and shadow, the subtle nuances of color, and the emotions conveyed through shape and form. After experimenting with all available choices, I felt most comfortable using acrylics and mixed media. I realized that art, like medicine, is a lifelong journey of learning, discovery, and evolution.

Finding My Purpose Through Art

As my skills grew as an artist, so did my desire to make a difference through this new medium. I began donating pieces for fundraisers that supported causes close to my heart—healing and soothing physically and mentally challenged patients, helping children with autism, protecting the environment, and women's empowerment. I started to create a series of paintings on these themes.

The art world is as competitive and challenging as the medical field, so I approached it with the same determination. I entered competitions, participated in exhibitions, and slowly began to carve out a niche for myself as an artist who creates healing artworks.

One of the most rewarding moments came during the COVID-19 pandemic. I responded to a call from The Washington Post for COVID-related art. My piece was listed among the top 20 in the nation. A year later, the Centers for Disease Control and Prevention (CDC) sought that same artwork for the cover of their Journal of Emerging Infectious Diseases. It was a moment of pure joy—my two worlds, medicine and art, coming together in perfect harmony.

The Healing Power of Art

My paintings now hang in hospitals for patients and their families to enjoy. They're displayed in colleges and private institutions, inspiring young minds. Each piece carries not just aesthetic value but also the potential to make a real difference in people's lives.

As I continue my artistic journey, I'm increasingly focused on spreading awareness about the healing power of art. Painting is a form of meditation for me. It allows me to process emotions, find calm in chaos, and connect with something greater than myself.

My journey from a renowned doctor to an award-winning artist has taught me valuable lessons:

Embrace change, even when it's forced upon us. It can lead to beautiful new beginnings.

Find your purpose. True fulfillment has come by aligning my work with my values. Never stop learning and evolving. Life is a continuous journey of growth.

Resilience is key. It has been my greatest asset throughout my life.

Balance tradition and personal values. I forge my path, while respecting my roots.

I would be remiss if I didn't acknowledge my biggest supporters—my family. My husband, our sons, their spouses and my grandchildren are my loudest cheerleaders, as is the encouragement of my extended family and friends. Without such a fanbase, progress would be difficult, and I feel truly blessed.

A Canvas Yet to Be Completed

As I look to the future, I'm filled with excitement and purpose. I have solo exhibitions planned, new techniques to explore, and countless ideas swirling in my mind. However, more than that, I have a message to share with my readers and the world. To anyone out there feeling stuck, unsure, or afraid to make a change—take that leap. Whether it is learning a new skill, changing careers, or simply exploring a long-forgotten passion, do it. The world needs your unique gifts, your experiences, and your perspective.

Remember, life isn't about avoiding risks; it's about taking the right ones. It's about continuously growing, learning, and finding new ways to make a positive impact on the world around us. My journey from the stethoscope to the paintbrush has been unexpected, challenging, and, ultimately, enormously rewarding. It's taught me that our potential for growth and reinvention is limitless. It's never too late to start a new chapter, to find a new way to heal oneself and the world.

So, what's your next chapter going to be? What hidden passions are waiting to be explored? What difference are you going to make in the world? The canvas of your life is waiting. It's time to pick up your brush and start painting.

Final Thoughts

If my story resonates with you, I invite you to explore how art can also transform your life.

Visit my website (www.VasuTolia.art) to see my latest works, learn about upcoming exhibitions, or inquire about ready or commissioned pieces that can bring healing and inspiration to your space. Let's connect and explore how art can be a force for positive change in your life and the world.

Dr. Vasundhara (Vasu) Tolia

Dr. Vasundhara (Vasu) Tolia is a remarkable individual who has successfully transitioned from a distinguished career in pediatric gastroenterology to become an award-winning artist. Born and raised in Kolkata, India, Dr. Tolia overcame societal constraints and political unrest to pursue her medical education. She immigrated to the United States, where she specialized in pediatric gastroenterology, becoming a pioneer in her field by establishing the first pediatric endoscopy unit at her institution.

Dr. Tolia rose to become a full tenured professor and division director, publishing over 150 papers and developing a fellowship program. Her commitment to excellence and self-motivation led her to become her own mentor, pushing the boundaries of her field.

Due to unexpected challenges in academia, she made the difficult decision to transition to private practice. This led to a journey of self-discovery, to explore the world of art. Despite initial struggles, she persevered, evolving from a novice to a skilled artist working primarily in acrylics and mixed media.

Her abstract and semi-abstract artworks, on themes of healing, women's empowerment, mental health, and environmental protection, are now displayed in hospitals and College Campus, providing comfort to many. During the COVID-19 pandemic, her artwork was featured by The Washington Post and later used by the CDC for a journal cover, bridging her medical background with her artistic pursuits.

Dr. Tolia continues to create art that raises awareness for various causes, including mental health, autism, environmental protection, and women's empowerment. Her journey exemplifies resilience, lifelong learning, and the power of reinvention. Through her art, she continues to heal, inspire, and connect with others, proving that the power of creativity is boundless. Dr. Tolia's story serves as an inspiration for those seeking to explore new passions and make a positive impact at any stage of life. Visit her website, (www.VasuTolia.art), to explore her latest works and learn more about her mission to blend art and healing.

Dr. Vasundhara (Vasu) Tolia
VasuToliaFineArt
Bloomfield Hills, MI
www.VasuTolia.art

Healing Art: Elevate Your Space with Art!

Discover the secrets to selecting and displaying art like a pro with my free guide: *How to Choose and Display Art for Maximum Impact.* Transform your home or office into a sanctuary of beauty and inspiration with tips that make hanging art simple and stunning.

Download your guide and explore more of my exclusive artworks. Let's create spaces that speak to the soul!

www.VasuTolia.art/howtochooseanddisplayartlikeapro

Shauna Van Mourik

You're Never Not Marketing: Stepping Into Your Authentic Power

Marketing Rebels—You're Never Not Marketing

I was warm—like too many glasses of a good red, warm—and shaking. Was I even breathing? As I mindlessly moved my little glass container of gold paperclips for the thirteenth time, I thought, "I can't do this..." Panic rose in my chest, and my heart raced to my throat. A waterfall roared in my ears, and the room blurred into a haze.

I was at a business event designed to elevate the visibility of women entrepreneurs. However, I wasn't just attending; I was a keynote speaker. I was surrounded by accomplished professionals who seemed to exude confidence effortlessly. Meanwhile, I felt like an imposter, as though I had somehow slipped through the cracks. This experience, and others like it, is part of what inspired me to write this book and develop a comprehensive program to help women navigate these challenges in their businesses.

Who was I to stand on that stage and speak about how to confidently grow a business using neuroscience, systems, and marketing? The irony of my self-doubt wasn't lost on me. The fact that I was supposed to be an expert in front of these people in just a few hours seemed irrelevant.

The whispers of doubt grew louder with each passing moment. "Do I belong here? Can I really make a difference? Will they even listen?" These questions echoed in my mind. With my usual side braid, yellow-gold summer dress, and boho faux leather boots, I stuck out like a sore thumb in this business-casual crowd.

The panic built slowly, then hit me all at once. I was just about to pack up my gold paperclips and leave, when a friendly face appeared in my peripheral vision. It was not someone I knew, but someone whose kindness and warmth were immediately apparent. She approached with small, confident steps and a gentle smile that felt like a lifeline.

She reminded me that confidence doesn't always come in loud, bold packages. Sometimes, it's quiet and reassuring, the kind that makes you feel seen and safe. Before I knew it, I was teary-eyed, spilling out my fears to this stranger who listened with genuine interest and empathy.

To my surprise, she found my fears and realizations deeply relatable and even thanked me for putting so many things into perspective for her. She wasn't surprised that I was chosen to speak and was eager to hear the insights I had to share.

As I expressed my gratitude, she hugged me with the warmth of someone who understands. I felt a little more like myself again—connected to what makes me, ME. I realized that confidence isn't about wearing a mask of self-assuredness. It is about having the courage to be my authentic self, quirks, and all.

That's why I chose this dress, these boots, and even this hairstyle. That's why I don't hold back my big expressions, hand gestures, and quirky humor. That's why I'm here and why these incredible women need to hear what I have to say!

As I released her reassuring hug, I also released the need to conform. I started showing up as the real me. As I did, I witnessed remarkable transformations. By being unapologetically myself, I attracted meaningful connections and found a wellspring of empowerment that fueled my actions and decisions from that moment on.

If you flipped through the pages of my life, you'd find more moments like this. There were moments when I doubted whether I was good enough, smart enough, or strong enough. You'd find chapters where I stumbled, where my confidence wavered, and where I questioned whether my voice mattered. However, you'd also find the turning points—where I faced my inner critic, chose courage over comfort, and decided to be authentically me.

This journey isn't just about personal growth; it's about showing up in your business with that same authenticity. It's about attracting clients who resonate with the real you, growing a business that reflects your true values, and making an impact by being the person you're meant to be.

Worthy

There are always freakin' rules.
Unspoken. Outspoken. Soft-spoken. Bespoken.
Reinforced, Implied, or Swept under the rug,
Under-the-table or right-in-your-face.
What to be, what to have, what to do, what to think, and even what to dream...
In order to be worthy.
Worthy of what, though?
The partner, the house, the car, the vacation... the success.
What if I told you, you are more than enough?

Who sticks a poem in the middle of a chapter? I do, because it's fun!

What's life without a little fun? This story isn't only about that, though, is it?

It's not just about personal liberation. It's about turning that freedom into business success. I've also developed a program that provides women life coaches and therapists with actionable strategies to align their personal values with their business goals, paving the way to true self-worth and sustainable growth.

For Now, Welcome

Welcome to a place where empowerment and authenticity exist alongside the unwavering belief that you have the capacity to choose your own path, making a profound impact on your life and the world around you.

Yes, you.

The one hiding behind a book whose title doesn't quite feel right (yet). The one who lives on the fringe of what others call "normal" (a dryer setting, in my opinion), balancing precariously between your true interests and what people say you should be doing. The one who notices what others miss thinks differently, and has ideas that are out of this world, large and in charge, heart fluttering, scary-exciting, and filled with passion… but no one knows it.

Overlooked, misunderstood, yet infinitely powerful—
You have found your sanctuary.
In the dance between your quirks and society's expectations, you're not alone.
Emerging from the shadows of conventional wisdom,
let's uncover the extraordinary.

This is a space where your uniqueness is not a liability but a superpower in both life and business. It's a haven for the dreamers, thinkers, and creators. They are the ones who believe in the magic of their ideas, even when the world hasn't caught up.

As a neuro-distinct, ultra-creative, neuroscience-obsessed, dreamer of an entrepreneur, I understand the struggle of existing between the lines. Those lines are a canvas for your self-expression. You're not defined by labels; you're celebrated for defying them.

You've felt the frustration of being overlooked and misunderstood. However, within these written words, your narrative takes center stage. In your business, that narrative has the power to attract clients who resonate with your true self, helping you grow a practice that's as unique as you are.

The world might not always grasp the magnitude of your ideas. However, here, they find a home. It is a space where they can breathe, evolve, and, ultimately, change the world.

This is not just another conceptual space with a self-help theme; it's a community, congregation, a conglomeration of amazing thought leaders who are hell-bent on discovering and nurturing the courage to be comfortably confident.

The mission? To unravel the secrets of comfortable confidence and create a space where every unique voice can resonate loud and clear.

In a world that often portrays confidence as a rare trait possessed by a select few, I want you to know that is a lie. Confidence is not about conforming to someone else's definition of it. It's about owning your unique identity. In your business, this means you don't need to mimic others to attract clients or make an impact; you just need to be authentically, unapologetically yourself.

Your quest for confidence, courage, and a lasting legacy is not a new one. We all share those moments when we question ourselves, when self-doubt whispers in our ears, and when life's challenges feel a bit too overwhelming.

I don't say this to disenchant you but rather to empower you. Together, we'll navigate the terrain of self-doubt, challenge the status quo, and uncover the incredible power that lies within you. It is the power to confidently create the life and business you envision and live it on your own terms.

Welcome to a place where your overlooked brilliance becomes the spark that ignites a revolution of authenticity, empowerment, and profound impact.

You were always worthy.
Worthy of what, though?
It all.

Before you call BS on my grande, optimistic declarations of self-worth, consider this lesson that I had to learn the hard way.

> *"Always keep the door of possibility open;*
> *you never know when an opportunity will walk in."*
>
> —Shauna L. Van Mourik

Yep, that's a me quote, and I'm very proud of it. This is not because it's in a book or because it holds profound meaning (even though it is and it does) but because it's true, real, and born from pain.

I loathe to admit how many times I let the world around me influence my choices in a way that closed the doors to my potential. I wanted to be an architect, a teacher, an interior designer, and an artist! But my math "wasn't good enough," there were "no jobs," I "wouldn't like looking at different shades of white," and I would inevitably wind up broke and starving... according to them.

While I don't regret where I wound up (I actually get to do all of these things in one way or another and more today), I do wish I had given myself permission to keep those doors open sooner. The opportunities that fuel my business and life today could have started years ago if I had embraced the possibility earlier.

Thinking back to the speaking gig I nearly ran away from: Imagine if I'd let fear and doubt win that day. Imagine if I'd packed up my golden paperclips and closed the door to the possibility of being a keynote speaker. Imagine if I chose not to empower those women, inspiring them to show up as only they can—to grow their businesses, attract their ideal clients, and make their unique impact.

I watched those women leave that event with ambitious goals, bold plans, and the mounting confidence to get it done. If I had closed my own door of possibility, I would have been inadvertently closing so many others—and we can't have that.

You see, my own journey, like yours, is one marked by an unbearable weight of self-doubt, where I constantly question my abilities, worthiness, and place in a world filled with expectations.

This Stuff Doesn't Just Go Away

Sometimes, in spite of your best efforts (or maybe because of them), what you want and what you need becomes confused and heavy. Then, what to DO and who to BE becomes overwhelming and seemingly impossible. This is often heaviest when you're just starting out in your business or reaching for that next big goal—and, I won't lie, it sucks!

However, don't fool yourself into thinking it will just go away when you reach your next milestone. We are meant to evolve and grow. These feelings will do the same. With each round of rebirth will come a new set of challenges. These obstacles will be so much easier to overcome when you have the confidence to keep your business doors open to possibility, to seize new opportunities, and to build a life and business filled with authentic power.

Confidence is not a static destination you reach and remain at indefinitely either. It's a dynamic journey, an ongoing relationship you nurture with yourself. It's about believing in your abilities, even when doubt looms on the horizon, and summoning the courage to take action, despite uncertainty.

It is not the absence of fear. It is the acceptance of it. It's not a shield that protects you from failure; it's a guiding light that leads you through some of your darkest moments. It's the fuel that propels you to seize opportunities, attract clients, grow your business, and create an impact that resonates far beyond yourself.

When I stopped trying to fit into someone else's mold and instead celebrated my own uniqueness, I found my voice, embraced my quirks, and became unapologetically myself. The most astonishing part was what happened next: My business began to flourish, opportunities unfolded, connections deepened, and my impact rippled through my community.

Remember that my journey began with courage, and so does yours—the courage to embrace your authentic self, to accept your imperfections, and to step confidently into the life and business you desire.

Carrying You Through This Adventure

A few themes that I want you to carry through this adventure are those of "Comfortable Confidence," "Grounded Luxury," and the fact that "You are never not marketing." These concepts are a cornerstone of my upcoming book as well as the backbone for the practical tools I share in my comprehensive marketing program. This is all designed to help you harness sustainable, results-driven marketing that feels good, ensuring that every interaction contributes positively to your brand's growth, client attraction, and personal journey.

The idea that you are never not marketing comes from psychology, the human condition, and my own journey in life and entrepreneurship. You see... when you show up in the world—whether in a line-up at the grocery store or on international TV—you are marketing. You're always sending a message out into the world, impacting those around you in ways that ripple far beyond the immediate moment. This means you have a responsibility attached to how you're showing up, both in your personal life and in your business.

This is also true when you wake up in the morning and see that stunning bedhead in the mirror. You are marketing to yourself as well, shaping your mindset and the way you approach your day. What you do, say, and think has an impact on your internal and external reality. Ask yourself, "What kind of day do I want to have today?" Use your marketing prowess to set the tone for success, in both life and business.

You Are Never Not Marketing

On the flip side is the fact that you are always being marketed to. That is, you are consistently receiving information from this complex world—and its inhabitants—around you. From this angle, you can understand that it is vital to think critically about how we receive and digest the information being fed to us.

Don't get me wrong, it's not all bad. There are many forms of this marketing that play a beneficial role in our personal development. The problem comes when we receive and embody messaging that is untrue or misaligned. When we retain this information about ourselves and the world around us, we wind up thinking, responding, and acting in ways that take us away from our potential.

Grounded Luxury

Grounded Luxury is not just a concept—it's a way of life that blends practicality with ambition, especially in your business. It's about finding that sweet spot where practicality and ambition coexist. It's about acknowledging the realities of life, while nurturing the audacious belief that you can achieve greatness.

Action is the bridge between imagination and reality, bringing the concept of grounded luxury vividly to life in your business. Grounded luxury isn't just about flashy, idealized notions; it's all about living a life that mixes being practical with dreaming big, making the ordinary days feel a bit more special. It acknowledges the raw truths of life—its limitations and challenges—while still daring to reach for greatness.

This philosophy encourages us to live fully in the present, appreciating the luxury of pursuing our dreams with both feet firmly on the ground. In business, it's about making decisions that reflect both where you are and where you aspire to be, understanding that true luxury lies in the ability to grow and scale your business, while staying true to your core values. It's the force that propels your thoughts and aspirations out of the realm of the abstract and into the tangible world. In this sense, action is not just a step but a commitment to bridging the gap between what is and what could be, making the concept of grounded luxury a lived experience in both your personal and professional life.

Remember that life is a delicate balance between ambition and presence. While your dreams propel you forward, it's in the art of being fully engaged in the present that you discover the beauty of "grounded luxury."

Comfortable Confidence

Comfortable Confidence is not just a buzzword; it's a philosophy, a way of life. It's about embracing your whole self, unapologetically. Here, you are encouraged to be the loud, the weird, the soft-spoken, the fangirling, the dirty-minded, the mathlete—whatever makes you, well, you. No more unreachable perfection. Instead, lean into the real and raw authenticity that will attract the right clients and opportunities to your business.

People will say...

> *"You know you're on the right track when it feels uncomfortable."*

I say...

> *"There's a fine line between living in your comfort zone and finding out what is (or isn't) in alignment with your authentic self."*

Learning the difference is about peeling away the layers of conditioning that have dictated your path and finding what truly resonates with your core, both in life and in business. Discomfort, in this context, isn't an obstacle; it's a signpost showing two distinct paths: 1. the push to venture further or 2. the nudge to pivot in a new direction. Deciphering this message requires introspection and courage.

A Word To The Wise

Your comfort zone is like a cozy blanket fort. It's warm, familiar, and reassuringly predictable. In this personal retreat, everything is in its place, and life unfolds with a reassuring rhythm—nothing changes, and the status quo continues onward.

Your sanctuary of safety can easily morph into a velvet prison, subtly dissuading you from pursuing the uncharted territories of your potential. We're not meant to live in enclosures, no matter how comfortable they may seem. We're built to run wild, to explore, and to discover our true power.

Becoming Comfortably Confident isn't about never stumbling; it's about moving forward with purpose, one step at a time. Each action you take builds your confidence and brings your dreams within reach. Remember, every small victory deserves celebration.

I want you to carry with you the understanding that action is the catalyst for change. Your dreams are not just dreams; they are possibilities waiting to be brought to life.

Keep That Door Open!

When you walk through it—embracing authenticity, confidence, and strategic action—remember that having comfortable confidence is the key to unlocking remarkable results in both your life and business. When you truly embrace who you are and show up confidently, you pave the way for profound positive changes.

Confidence is a powerful catalyst for transformation. When you stand tall in your authentic power, you attract opportunities, build meaningful connections, and achieve your goals with ease. Your comfortable confidence fuels your actions and propels you toward the success you envision.

To support you on this journey, I've created a resource designed to help you balance life's demands with your entrepreneurial spirit: The Dream Business, Dream Life RoadMap —your ultimate guide to mastering your time, prioritizing self-compassion, and achieving your business goals with ease.

Ready to transform the way you approach your days—both personally and professionally? The Dream Business, Dream Life RoadMap is not just another planner; it's a 12-week guide specifically crafted for women in business.

This map helps you plot out not just your business tasks, but also those moments that matter most in life:

- Big Launches
- Business Development
- Client Work

- Everyday Obstacles
- Vacation!

The Dream Business, Dream Life RoadMap, has you covered.

It's time to step out of the shadows and into the spotlight. This resource is more than just tips. It's a guide to elevate your brand and make sure your voice is heard. Ready to shine? Dive into the RoadMap and watch your brand and business transform.

Let's create a life together where you confidently show up as your authentic self, embrace your unique path, attract amazing clients, and make a profound impact. When you cultivate and harness your confidence, you open doors to extraordinary possibilities and a fulfilling, successful life.

Shauna Van Mourik

An advocate for positively impacting the world, Shauna creates a space where ambitious women feel comfortably confident leading authentically and inspiring ripples in their communities. As a business strategist, Shauna uses organic growth marketing to help women, life coaches, and therapists attract aligned clients who are ready and excited to invest. She dives deep, asks tough questions, and leverages their unique personal brands to grow their business beyond six figures. Psychology-based, goal-oriented, and people-focused, Shauna believes that marketing confidence makes a difference and that it not only has to convert but also feel good.

Shauna Van Mourik
SLA Marketing Confidence
Ontario, Canada
Shauna@ShaunaLeigh.com
www.ShaunaLeigh.com

Dream Business, Dream Life RoadMap

Are you ready to stop spinning your wheels and start building a business you love—without sacrificing your personal life? The Dream Clients, Dream Life RoadMap is a powerful 12-week guide designed to help women entrepreneurs achieve their biggest business goals while mastering time, avoiding burnout, and creating a lifestyle they love.

This isn't just another planner—it's your step-by-step blueprint to balancing personal fulfillment with professional success. From planning big launches and attracting dream clients to managing everyday challenges and prioritizing rest, this RoadMap covers it all.

Whether you prefer a digital tool or a pen-and-paper approach, this RoadMap has everything you need to make progress with ease. Plus, the bonus 13th week ensures you never miss a beat, giving you space to reflect and strategize for your next 12 weeks.

Ready to build your dream business and live the life you love?

Get instant access to the Dream Clients, Dream Life RoadMap and start your journey toward sustainable success today!

www.ShaunaLeigh.com/DreamBusiness-DreamLife-Roadmap

Carla Lewis

Inside the Fishbowl: Navigating Leadership and Change

Fishbowl Fallout: An Unexpected Reckoning

"YOU! GET UP HERE!"

The command hit me like a punch, slicing through the hum of machinery that vibrated the floors in the bowels of this manufacturing facility.

It was Monday, September 10, 1979. I stood alone in an elevated glass-walled office, like a fishbowl, exposed to the glare of sixteen angry men below, every pair of eyes sharp and suspicious.

In their world, **I** was the threat.

I felt vulnerable—a 25-year-old computer programmer. Female. These men—some who had worked longer than I'd been alive—were seething because of a computer report I'd written that seemed to render parts of their work redundant. While simply data to me, for them, it was an assault on their routines, their roles, and even their sense of purpose.

"How can we trust the report?" one demanded, his voice laden with skepticism. "And now what?" another barked, his question weighted with fear. "If this report does it all... then who am I?"

Their unspoken concern hit me like a freight train: What am I worth if this report renders me obsolete?

The walls felt as if they were closing in. At that moment, I realized I had but one choice: to step forward, even without all the answers.

I straightened my jacket, smoothed my skirt, and spoke, my voice steady, even if only on the surface. "Let's walk through this together," I said. "We'll trace the data to its source and figure out how it supports you in the work you are already doing."

The factory noise softened as if a curtain had dropped, creating a space where we could bridge the divide—not just with data but with a willingness to confront change together.

Curious Beginnings: Shaping a Leader in Change

My story begins with two powerful forces: a mother who defied expectations and a father who nurtured curiosity.

My engineer father was all about the inner workings of radios and televisions. He welcomed me into his world of circuits and signals, sparking my love for technology. He taught me not just to observe but to understand how things worked. It was my earliest lesson in curiosity and problem-solving.

My mother was unstoppable. What began as a hobby in photography became a business. Her cameras caught beautiful beginnings mirrored in weddings and births. She also documented endings found in accidents, fires, and crime scenes for the Detroit area police and fire departments. Not stopping there, she became a licensed pilot in 1967—a rare feat for women in that era—and later added master mechanic to her resume. She was fearless, determined, and relentless. She was the life force that molded me.

In this setting, I grew up knowing few limits. My love for math and problem-solving emerged early, and it wasn't long before I discovered the magic of computer programming. For me, programming was problem-solving at its purest—a puzzle I couldn't resist.

In college, a professor sponsored me for a data entry job, supporting my education and giving me valuable experience. After 18 full-time months, I returned to school, this time diving into organizational psychology. I had no idea why at the time, but it would prove to be the piece I didn't know I needed.

One year later, my application for a summer job in a data center led to a full-time programming position! It was my big break, my chance to step fully into the world of technology. And from my first day, I realized I was in uncharted territory.

Corporate America in the 1970s was no place for a woman in a technical role. I was one of the first non-secretarial women hired. There were no rules for how women should behave in that environment. The men had no experience with women as peers. We were writing the rules as we went along. To survive, I quickly learned to balance assertiveness with diplomacy in an environment where every step was scrutinized.

My career advanced steadily, with each role bringing new experiences and opportunities to work with teams across continents and functions. I wasn't just programming—I was leading organizations through complex technology transformations. We weren't simply installing software; we were changing the way people worked, reshaping processes, and forcing teams to adapt. I knew the real challenge lay not in the code but in the people impacted by it. The real work wasn't in the programming but in preparing people for change.

Every initiative demanded answers to complex questions: *What's changing? Who will it impact? How will we support them through it?* These answers, not just the technical steps, would determine success or failure.

The early days were tough—they were also defining. In my first performance review, despite my hard work and technical success, I was rated satisfactory. The feedback stung, especially the part where my manager said, "You smile too much. You'll never get anywhere in this company if you keep smiling."

Well, I didn't stop smiling. And I didn't stop working. Instead, I doubled down, focusing on mastering both the technical and human sides of change.

My career progressed, and eventually, I rose to the top 2% of leadership across the company. The only interview I ever had was the one that got me in the door. Each role taught me something new. However, the ultimate lesson was clear: Technology is only as effective as the people who use it.

I realized that every experience I had was building toward something larger. My father's love for engineering, my mother's fierce independence, my journey through global technology transformations, and even that fateful day in the 'fishbowl'—all these moments led me to one powerful epiphany: **Leadership accountability for organizational readiness is the key to successful change.**

Technology evolves, and organizations need leaders who can navigate transformation's technical and human sides. That realization, combined with 45 years of hands-on experience in technology and organizational change management, led me to develop what I now call the Roadmap to Readiness Assessment and Strategy.

I now guide leaders through comprehensive assessments to profile the impact of change on their people, processes, and operations. We build executable plans together, with each leader understanding their role in leading through change and driving success.

My mission is simple yet profound: to help leaders save time, money, and the inevitable drama that comes with changing how people work. Leaders who understand their accountability and step fully into their responsibility are the ones who ignite real, lasting success.

I envision a future where every project that changes how people work starts with the Roadmap to Readiness Assessment. It's a world where leaders are always ready to lead through change with confidence. That future remains my mission.

My Lightbulb Moment

September 10, 1979—a day that split my career and my life into Before and After.

That day, I was thrust from the back office of data processing into the center ring of information technology's assault on the workplace.

I stood at the crossroads of data and disruption, watching as technology collided with entrenched processes, creating chaos. Leaders had no roadmap to guide people through such rapid change—no way to prepare teams for a shift that would alter workflows and identities.

At that moment, I realized that the core issue wasn't the technology itself. It was the lack of support for the people impacted by it. However, management brushed my insight aside. *"Carla, we do data, not people."*

Oh yeah?!?

If they couldn't see the importance, I would prove it. Determined, I pursued degrees, certifications, and a deeper understanding of human behavior and leadership. Over the next 40+ years, I honed my craft, creating tools, coaching leaders, and building a movement that brought the human element together with technology.

From Data to Destiny: Defining a New Leadership Path

Determined to answer the questions management ignored—how to support people through change—I threw myself into the pursuit of knowledge. If leadership was the missing link, I needed to master it. If organizational change was the problem, I needed to understand it from every angle.

I earned a B.A. in Management of Human Resources from Spring Arbor University. My real-world experience in the Planned Change Internship taught me to navigate the delicate interplay between people and processes, showing me that resistance to change wasn't just inevitable—it was manageable with the right strategies.

Eager to deepen my expertise, I pursued an M.S. in Human Resource Development at The American University, immersing myself in the complexities of organization development. Studying Organizational Learning with MIT's Dr. Peter Senge integrated a transformational perspective on how organizations grow and evolve.

Certifications followed—PROSCI Organizational Change Management Practitioner, Life Optimization Coach—each adding a layer to my expertise and the frameworks I designed and leveraged with leaders globally.

My mentors—visionaries like Kathleen Dannemiller, Dr. Peter Senge, Peter Block, and Dr. Carol Anderson—showed me that organizational success isn't about systems but the hearts and minds of people who implement them.

Over the next 40+ years, I refined my approach, developed tools, and coached managers on leading through change. I developed a superpower—bridging the gap between transformation's technical and human components. My journey was recognized with a Lifetime Achievement Award, a Wall Street Journal Distinguished Leader honor, and a 2024 Marquis Who's Who induction, reflecting not just skills but a legacy built through grit, determination, and grace.

These accomplishments are not just titles and accolades. They prove that I've walked the path, and I now guide others. Change is inevitable. Success requires preparation, leadership, and courage. I now help leaders build trust, manage resistance, and ignite success with strategy and vision.

Forged in Adversity: The Cost of Ambition

From the start, I knew that my pursuit wouldn't come without sacrifice. However, I didn't realize just how much going after it would cost me financially, emotionally, and physically.

When I set my sights on earning my master's degree, I was told the company didn't recognize the need I was seeking to meet. While I saw the studies as strengthening my contributions, they were dismissed as unworthy of tuition assistance because *"I.T. people have no business worrying about people's stuff."* That rejection merely fueled my resolve.

I was accepted into the program and jumped into the two-year circus of balancing work, travel, classes, research, studies, and regular life. This involved monthly trips to Washington, D.C., each weekend involving three days of intense coursework. I paid for school, books, flights, hotels, and meals on my own. To make it all work, I negotiated with my boss to work a 40- to 50-hour week compressed into four days monthly.

It was relentless, draining, and physically demanding. The experience shaped me, teaching me about perseverance, dedication, and the importance of a support system. My partner, family, and friends stood by me and made it possible, a lifeline in the darkest moments.

Meanwhile, the workplace presented its own set of challenges. Because I was single, management assumed I had no personal life. I was often assigned to the most demanding projects because, in their words, *"You don't have a life that would interfere."* Boundaries weren't an option. If they needed someone available around the clock, that someone was me.

Even the basics of having a workspace were a challenge. My first manager's office was a desk in the hallway, right next to the shared printer. From the hallway, I was moved to a conference table shared with four people—no phone, no desk drawers, just a table. I learned to stay organized out of necessity, carrying everything I needed with me. When that space was repurposed, my office became... my car.

When I finally landed an office, it was a converted closet deep in an old building, retrofitted with lights, ventilation, and the essentials. However, by then, I had learned that success wasn't about where you worked—it was about how you showed up. And I always showed up.

The hard work led to a promotion to a division operating committee as head of I.T. and other service functions—a role with a large office, a conference table, and its own bathroom! Things shifted after a year, and I was moved to a smaller office at the end of the main hall. The trappings of success in a corporate environment are never permanent and never guaranteed.

To complicate things further, I was placed in a matrix reporting relationship—reporting to both the I.T. and manufacturing divisions.

Delivering for two masters with competing priorities was a balancing act. The burden of keeping both sides happy was daunting. It was exhausting, yet it taught me diplomacy, time management, and resilience.

After nearly 30 years with the company, I sensed a shift—subtle but undeniable. There was a distancing from leadership and a growing sense that my value was being questioned. While I wasn't done making a difference, I could see the writing on the wall. I decided to retire on my terms. I didn't want to wait to be ushered out—I left with my head held high, knowing that I had given everything I had.

These experiences weren't just lessons; they were the foundation of my expertise. Every struggle and every challenging assignment shaped how I approach my work today. I learned that navigating change without the proper support is costly and exhausting and that leaders who embrace change with courage and a plan achieve remarkable success.

That's why I do what I do. I know what it feels like to go it alone and how much smoother the journey can be with the proper guidance. I now help leaders avoid the mistakes that have already been made. Because while the weeds are inevitable, no one should have to tackle them alone.

The Leadership Forge: Shaping Resilience and Influence

The journey wasn't just about overcoming obstacles but about becoming stronger and more capable. Every challenge I faced, and every setback I endured added a new layer to who I was becoming as a thought leader. The skills I developed along the way weren't just about survival; they became the foundation for the tools and frameworks I now use to help others lead through change.

The first and perhaps most crucial lesson I learned was resilience and perseverance. Earning my master's degree without support from my company tested my endurance in ways I didn't anticipate. Every late-night flight and every weekend spent balancing coursework with work deadlines sharpened my resolve. It taught me that the only way out of adversity is through it. This sense of resilience became the bedrock of my leadership style—I knew how to keep moving forward, no matter how steep the challenge.

I also honed skills in leadership and people management. Managing complex teams and navigating organizational politics developed my empathy, patience, and ability to recognize potential in others—even when they couldn't see it themselves. I learned that leadership isn't about authority; it's about influence and trust. These lessons became the core of my coaching practice, where I help leaders find their voice and guide their teams through uncertainty.

The most transformative skills I developed are adaptability and resourcefulness. Every inconvenience, political challenge, and demanding project forced me to innovate and find creative solutions. This fuels the entrepreneurial mindset that now powers my mission.

Tips for Your Journey: Beliefs in Action

1. Embrace Change

Approach change as an opportunity to grow and evolve. Success lies in adaptability.

2. Leverage Support Systems

Build a network of allies who uplift you during challenges.

3. Develop Resilience

View setbacks as stepping stones and respond from your core of strength and humility.

Through these experiences, I became the leader I am today, helping others navigate change and emerge stronger. This journey taught me that while challenges are unavoidable, they are the proving grounds of greatness. If I can overcome them, so can you.

The Leadership Horizon: Building Legacies of Impact

My journey has taken me across decades, industries, and transformations. From that first retirement, I set out as an independent consultant, driven by my passion for helping organizations navigate change.

Consulting projects and incredible partnerships led from there to the highlight of my corporate America experience, where I worked with a dream team doing dream work for a dream senior executive.

We tackled complex transformations together, blending technology and people into solutions that worked—not just on paper but in practice. It was glorious, and it, too, came to an end when I had given the organization all it could consume.

With that, I returned to my roots—independent coaching and consulting—now with an even greater sense of purpose and a clearer mission.

While one-on-one consulting remains part of my work, scaling my impact is the next step. There are only so many hours in a day—and only so much of me to go around. That's why I've embraced the role of speaker and educator, spreading the message of leadership in organizational readiness to all who will listen.

My mission is to empower leaders to confidently navigate change, fostering an environment where technology and humanity flourish together.

Join me in transforming organizational change into the goal it represents: organizational readiness.

Download my free "Concise Companion for Navigating Business Process Change." This high-value resource provides strategies to ensure your leadership plans exceed expectations. It serves as your guide to successfully navigating business process transformations.

Join me in navigating the nuances of change, crafting a future where adaptive leaders inspire, empowered teams excel, and organizations achieve unparalleled success.

Let's unleash your mastery!

The time for action is now. Let's create something extraordinary—together.

Carla Lewis

Carla Lewis helps leaders save time and money and the inevitable drama accompanying change in business process. Throughout her four plus decades leading, developing, teaching, and coaching for organizational readiness, Carla has helped hundreds of leadership teams succeed in business process transformation while maintaining their laser focus on managing day-to-day business demands.

In addition to her qualifications and experience as a Leadership and Organizational Change Strategist, Carla is an Award-winning Speaker, Certified Change Management Practitioner, Certified Life Optimization Coach, Podcast co-host, Honored Listee in Marquis Who's Who 2024, Marquis Lifetime Achievement Award winner, and celebrated 2024 Distinguished Leader in the Wall Street Journal.

Carla J. Lewis
CJL Innovations
Novi, MI
Carla@CJLInnovations.com

Navigate Change Now: The Essentials Guide For Leading With Confidence

In the fast-paced world of business, staying ready for change is vital. This handy and concise guide gives leaders the straightforward tools they need to align their organization for success. By focusing on the essentials of business and people readiness, it offers clear insights and easy-to-follow strategies for managing change effectively. Get your team prepared to tackle the challenges of shifting business processes and thrive. Discover practical tips and streamlined approaches that will help your organization stay ahead and flourish in times of change.

https://carlajlewis.com/navchgnowdwnld

Shellie Seyfarth, PhD

Emerging from the Grind:
Reclaiming a Life that Matters

A Legacy of Presence

The soft hum of whispered conversations echoed off the chapel's stained glass windows, filling the stillness with a muted, reverent hush. Outside, a heavy, overcast sky made the late afternoon feel like twilight, casting a somber light through the room. The air inside was thick with the scent of lilies, mingling with the weight of grief. I sat in the front row, hands folded in my lap, my gaze fixed on the casket that held my grandfather—the man who had been a quiet pillar of strength and integrity in our family for as long as I could remember.

As the minister's words filled the room, my mind wandered back through my memories of him. He was the embodiment of presence—steady, hardworking, the kind of person who showed up without fanfare. He never missed a family gathering, always offering quiet support that made you feel safe and valued. My grandfather believed that a person's worth wasn't measured by their accomplishments or titles, but by the way they treated others. His life was a testament to this, a reflection of values that felt timeless. His strength, understated yet unwavering, had always been there in the background of my life, an anchor I didn't realize I'd leaned on so heavily. Now, as he lay before us, gone, I felt the immensity of his absence.

As I sat there, a realization crept in that made my chest tighten. While he had always lived by these principles, my own life felt miles away from this kind of integrity and balance. My family nucleus had always been different—driven by success, achievement, and the relentless pursuit of being the best. I followed that path with a single-minded focus, driven by the belief that success was measured in hard work and accolades. As I looked around at the people gathered in his memory, I couldn't ignore the emptiness his passing left behind. I couldn't help but wonder: what kind of legacy was I building?

The contrast struck me with a painful clarity. If I continued on my current path, constantly sacrificing my own well-being and relationships for work, I knew what lay ahead. A life built on achievements and devoid of fulfillment. At that moment, sitting in the pew, surrounded by people who had loved him for who he was—not what he accomplished—I knew something had to change. My grandfather's life wasn't just a memory; it was a message, a call to realign with what truly mattered. I resolved, right then and there, that I would find a way to honor my grandfather's legacy by being a leader who chose connection over status, authenticity over appearances, and to create a life that honored his legacy of authenticity, integrity, and presence.

Born to Be Bold

Looking back, it's clear that I was raised to be fearless. Growing up with a mother who instilled a "you can do anything boys can do" mindset, I didn't see limitations—only possibilities. There were no different rules for my brother and me, no expectations that I should "play it small." I was an adventurous kid, a whirlwind of energy, always on the move. There wasn't a sport or activity I didn't throw myself into with full force. I knew I was smart and athletic, often captain of my teams, and I confidently embraced it.

When I entered the workforce, I carried that same boldness. I was determined to be productive, successful, and unapologetically ambitious. At first, it felt like a winning combination. I was known for getting things done, pushing limits, and going above-and-beyond. I quickly learned that boldness in a woman was often met with a different response. My male colleagues were admired for their confidence, while I was labeled as being "intimidating" or "difficult."

The bias wasn't just subtle; it was sometimes blatant. One day, a male manager asked me to run a report. I agreed, wanting to deliver the best work possible. On his way out, he asked my male colleague, "Could you run the same report to make sure she does it right?" I froze. Despite my spotless track record, my work was doubted simply because I was a woman. It was one of those small, infuriating moments that reminded me how high the stakes were and how much harder I'd have to work to prove myself.

Then there was the incident I'd never forget. I was hanging up my coat, mentally preparing for the day, when out of nowhere, a male leader walked up behind me and grabbed my chest. Without thinking, I reacted. My fist connected with his jaw before I registered what was happening. I could feel all eyes on me, but I didn't care. My heart was pounding, and I was shaking with anger—not just at him, but at all the times I had been brushed aside, belittled, or ignored.

It Was What Happened Next That Shocked Me Most

In the HR meeting that followed, I sat across from my boss and the HR rep, waiting for some semblance of justice, for some acknowledgment that what had just happened to me was wrong. Instead, I was reprimanded. **Me.** I was told my reaction had been "unprofessional." As for the man who violated me? He faced no consequences. Not even a slap on the wrist. It was as if it never happened. I was left with the bitter truth that protecting myself came with consequences.

That moment changed something in me. I knew the corporate world was tough, but this? This was a different kind of tough. It was a system rigged against me, one that would never see me as an equal no matter how hard I worked. However, I stayed. I kept coming back, day after day, telling myself that if I just worked harder, if I just played the game a little longer, things would change. I kept saying yes to every project, every request, and every late-night meeting, hoping that eventually, someone would notice and the respect would follow.

My personal life started to crumble under the weight of my career. I missed family dinners and skipped out on important events, always with the excuse that work was more important. "It's temporary," I'd tell myself. "Once I hit that next promotion or finish this project, I'll have time to breathe;" that breath never came.

I was running on fumes. I was constantly tired, rarely sleeping more than a few hours a night. I told myself it was the price of success, that everyone felt this way. Deep down, I knew I was heading in the wrong direction. The longer I kept this up, the more I lost sight of who I was and who I was meant to be.

I couldn't ignore the glaring inequities or the dismissiveness directed at women in the workplace. I started listening to stories from other women, their shared experiences of bias, condescension, and the constant need to prove their worth. Gradually, my curiosity about human behavior turned from a passing interest into a deep-seated passion, a drive to understand why women were often treated differently for the same accomplishments.

Determined to make a difference, I shifted my career from quality engineering into the people side of business. I threw myself into studying and earned my master's degree in Organizational Management, followed by a PhD in Industrial/Organizational Psychology. My curiosity turned into a passion for understanding the inner workings of behavior, motivation, and workplace dynamics. I added hundreds of hours of learning—and took on assignments that opened doors to international experiences. I was on a path to leadership, gathering expertise and perspective from every angle.

From the outside, I had it all. I traveled, worked long hours, and filled my schedule with competitive sports, friendships, and dating. Beneath it all, I felt a growing disconnect, an imbalance I couldn't ignore. I realized that "success" had come with a hidden cost. I was missing time with friends, often arriving late or canceling plans, and I was increasingly absent from the life I once loved. Little by little, I was trading pieces of myself for work's sake.

And for what? The companies I'd given my all to didn't see me as anything more than a resource, easily replaced. My sacrifices went unnoticed, and my achievements were hollow without a personal connection or purpose. The burnout crept up slowly, leaving me drained and disillusioned. I knew something had to change if I wanted a life of meaning. As I sat in that pew at my grandfather's funeral, surrounded by people who loved him for his unwavering presence, I understood that my ambition alone would never create the legacy I desired.

A Glimpse of What Could Be Lost

In the quiet after the funeral, I found myself alone, lost in thought. My grandfather's life left an undeniable mark on me: his quiet strength, his values, his unwavering presence for those he loved. It was clear that he hadn't measured his worth in titles or accolades. He'd measured it in moments, in the connections he built, and in the family he nurtured. As I thought about the life I was building, a wave of clarity hit me, piercing and undeniable.

If I kept going down this path—sacrificing so much—what kind of legacy would I leave? I'd climbed high and achieved much, but the emptiness behind those accomplishments was beginning to feel insurmountable. I could see where my choices were leading, and it was a life of relentless pursuit with little room for true fulfillment.

The realization was startling. For all my achievements, I knew that without a change, I'd be left with a life defined by work, not meaning. In that moment, I resolved to reclaim my path, to realign my priorities, and to build a life that, like my grandfather's, would be remembered for its integrity, balance, and purpose.

Building a New Foundation

After that day, the shift began. I knew I couldn't keep living a life so out of sync with who I wanted to be. I needed to create a foundation that aligned with my values—a foundation I could use for myself and to help others navigate these same struggles. My journey started with an intense commitment to learning and reorienting my purpose around understanding people, their motivations, and the dynamics that shape our lives and careers.

I dove into the research of human behavior, leadership, and resilience, driven by a need to create meaningful change. Knowledge became my grounding force. I sought certifications that broadened my perspective: women's empowerment, leadership coaching, executive coaching, life coaching, change management, communication, and even weightloss coaching. Each one gave me new tools, insights, and ways to connect with those who felt as I once had—stuck in a cycle of proving themselves, unable to step back and prioritize their well-being. It wasn't just about the credentials but the transformation happening within me.

Gradually, I felt the weight lifting. I learned to set boundaries that honored my values, to say "no" without guilt, and to finally put my needs on par with my achievements. My boundaries became non-negotiable, and my voice steadier. I started to embody the very resilience I hoped to inspire in others. I began journaling, reflecting daily on my actions, and checking in with myself to stay aligned with what mattered most. Each step helped me build the foundation of Emerging You—a path that wasn't just about my growth but empowering others to reclaim their lives and live purposefully. This path became my calling, and I knew I could guide others on this path.

Navigating the Weeds

The journey of transforming my life was a winding path filled with setbacks, moments of doubt, and countless reminders of how easy it is to slip back into old habits.

One moment stands out vividly. I was dating someone then, and we had plans to go out one evening. As we finalized our evening plans, he said, "You might need to wait for me." I jokingly said, "What? You want me to wait for you? I wait for no one!" I laughed. He didn't. He looked at me, frustration clear in his eyes, and said, "Do you know how many times I've waited for you? All the nights you were late, the times you didn't show up because of work, tennis, or some other commitment. I feel like I'm always waiting for you to show up."

His words stopped me cold. For so long, I'd thought my dedication and drive were positive traits that defined me. Yet here was someone I cared about, telling me that my constant prioritization of work and other responsibilities was leaving him—and, honestly, others—feeling undervalued. I apologized, but that moment stuck with me. I began to see that real change wasn't just about setting boundaries; it was about understanding the impact those choices had on the people in my life.

Determined to keep moving forward, I set firmer boundaries. I turned down late-night projects, reclaimed my weekends, and even left the office earlier than I used to. Not everyone understood. Some questioned whether my commitment had changed. Some dismissed it as a phase. It was easy to slip back into saying "yes" to one more project, another favor, or one more late night. Each setback reminded me how deeply ingrained these habits were—and how hard it would be to change them alone.

I reached out to a mentor. She listened without judgment and gently reminded me that my goals could align with a life of balance and fulfillment and that I didn't have to choose between success and self-respect. She helped me reframe my vision of success, not as constant productivity but as intentional, meaningful work that allowed room for life. Together, we worked through my tendencies to overcommit and the habit of putting myself last. It was frustrating, often exhausting work, and each step forward sometimes felt followed by two steps back.

Close friends were also there for me. They'd seen me at my best and at my worst. They weren't afraid to remind me of the person I was outside of my achievements. Their support kept me steady, their belief in me reinforced my belief in myself.

I returned to the hobbies I loved and made time for rebuilding relationships I hadn't nurtured. I began to see the rewards of staying true to my boundaries, of choosing connection over productivity. With each small success, I became more resilient and more aligned with the life I wanted to lead.

The journey wasn't without pain. It taught me that trying to go it alone had only prolonged my struggles. Every stumble reinforced my resolve to help others navigate their own paths with the support they needed. If there's one thing my journey taught me, it's that no one should have to fight through the weeds alone.

My Strategies

Through all the setbacks, growth, and hard-won victories, I emerged with a new set of tools that became my anchors. I had transformed, not only as a person but as a leader and entrepreneur. These strategies became my guiding principles, the tools that helped me reclaim my life and build a future based on purpose, respect, and resilience.

1. Setting Boundaries

Learning to set boundaries was one of my hardest and most rewarding changes. I discovered that saying "no" wasn't a weakness; it was an act of self-respect and self-care. Boundaries became my way of protecting my energy and time, allowing me to focus on what truly mattered. Over time, people saw that my "no" was firm, and my "yes" was fully committed.

2. Trusting My Gut

For years, I silenced my intuition, prioritizing others' expectations over my own inner wisdom. As I worked through my journey, I started listening to my gut. That trust brought me a confidence I hadn't realized I'd been missing. I learned that my intuition was my strongest compass, guiding me toward decisions aligned with my values and long-term vision.

3. Engaging in Self-Reflection

Every day, I took a moment to reflect. Asking myself a simple question: *"Were my words and actions worthy of respect?"* This practice kept me grounded, helping me align my actions with my values and make adjustments when I strayed. Self-reflection became a way to celebrate growth and course-correct, keeping me on the path I wanted to walk.

These tools didn't just help me through my own journey; they transformed me, allowing me to live a life of authenticity, balance, and fulfillment. I now use these same strategies to help others who are ready to reclaim their lives and live from a place of confidence and clarity.

A Life Reclaimed

Today, my life feels worlds away from what it once was. I've created a life where I wake up every morning feeling in control, fulfilled, and at peace with choices I make. I've reconnected with people who matter most, carved out time for golf, pickleball, family, and—perhaps most importantly—myself. My days are balanced between the work I love and the life I want, allowing me to support others without sacrificing my own well-being.

Getting here took years of learning, changing, and sometimes stumbling. Every step taught me what I needed to know—not just for myself but for those who find themselves in a similar place. My vision is to help others find this same freedom, reclaim their lives, set meaningful boundaries, and build futures that reflect their true worth.

If my story resonates with you—if you've ever felt overwhelmed, stretched too thin, like you're constantly being pulled in every direction but your own—then I invite you to take the first step toward change. You don't have to go through this alone, and you don't have to waste years figuring it out the hard way, like I did.

I've created a free resource specifically for people who are ready to set boundaries, trust their instincts, and build a life of self-respect. It's a simple, practical guide that will give you tools to begin making changes today.

You've already taken the first step by reading my story. Now, I invite you to take the next one—toward a life that's truly yours.

Shellie Seyfarth, PhD

Shellie Seyfarth, PhD, is a seasoned leadership coach and the founder of Emerging You, LLC, where she empowers high-achieving women to reclaim their lives and lead with confidence, clarity, and integrity. With over two decades of experience, Shellie has a unique background in Industrial/Organizational Psychology and multiple coaching certifications, equipping her with both the expertise and empathy to guide clients through challenges, like imposter syndrome, boundary-setting, and burnout. Her own journey, marked by relentless ambition and the eventual realization of the hidden costs of "the grind," has shaped her mission to help women find balance and fulfillment without sacrificing success.

Through Emerging You, Shellie's programs inspire clients to rediscover their core values, trust their intuition, and design boundaries that honor their well-being. Her clients don't just receive guidance—they gain a transformative toolkit for aligning their careers with their lives in ways that resonate with purpose and authenticity. Known for her down-to-earth style and genuine approach, Shellie believes true leadership stems from living in alignment with one's values, cultivating resilience, and embracing a life that matters.

Whether coaching executives or guiding women returning to the workforce, Shellie's work is a call to emerge from the grind and step into a life defined by integrity, connection, and self-worth.

Shellie Seyfarth, PhD
Emerging You, LLC
Dearborn, MI
Coach@EmergingYou.com
www.EmergingYou.com

Emerging You:
100 Power Thoughts to Reclaim Your Life

This powerful guide is designed for high-achieving women ready to break free from self-doubt, set meaningful boundaries, and lead a life aligned with their true purpose. You'll find 100 carefully crafted thoughts that empower you to reconnect with your inner strength, build confidence, and reclaim a life that's fully yours. Start each day with a thought that inspires resilience, clarity, and growth—your journey to a balanced and fulfilling life begins here.

Download your free copy today and take the first step toward reclaiming the life that you were meant to live.

https://subscribepage.io/XPAH9n

Julie Caprera

Willing to Be Willing: A Leap of Faith and Love

A Whisper of Fear and Possibility

The sun streamed through my sister's kitchen windows onto the table where we sat, enjoying our coffee. As I looked at my sister, my pulse quickened. Weeks ago, she had shared with me on a phone call something that was still echoing in my mind: **We've started homeschooling.**

At the time, I was floored. Homeschooling? The word conjured up images of isolation, boring textbooks, and children missing critical opportunities. I wasn't able to hide my skepticism. Now, here I was, visiting my sister to meet my new nephew and to learn more about what this decision actually meant.

My sister's eyes were filled with a quiet conviction. "It's not as strange as you think," she said, responding to my unspoken doubts. "We're figuring it out one day at a time, and it's already making a difference. It's working for us."

The next few days, I asked every question I could imagine about homeschooling. My sister's calm, thoughtful answers starkly contrasted with the whirlwind of doubts in my mind. She handed me two books by Dr. Raymond Moore: *Home Grown Kids* and *Home-Spun Schools*.

"These will explain a lot," my sister told me. "They were a game changer for me."

I spent hours reading. My emotions swirled between disbelief and curiosity. The stories in the books captivated me. These weren't perfect families or professional educators. They were ordinary parents stepping into the unknown with nothing but determination and a desire to give their children something more.

In one chapter, a mother described how she tailored her children's learning to fit their interests and strengths, turning daily activities into educational moments. Another chapter detailed the lifelong bonds forged within families who chose this path. The honesty of the stories struck a chord within me. Their words conveyed their passion, fear, and uncertainty—emotions I was feeling in myself.

Although there wasn't much formal teaching to observe during my visit, I watched my sister read to her preschool-aged daughter. The simple act was transformative in its own way. My sister wasn't just reading. She was cultivating a connection, showing her daughter that *learning could be joyful and intimate.*

As the visit drew to a close, I felt a knot forming in my stomach. The books, the conversations, and my sister's steadfast belief had sparked something in me—a tiny flicker of possibility I couldn't ignore.

Flying home, I wrestled with the question that refused to leave my mind: **Was I willing to be willing?** It wasn't a question of capability. Before pursuing a career as a nurse, I considered becoming a teacher. I was confident I could figure out the mechanics of homeschooling. *The real battle was whether I was ready to leave the known behind.*

Could I walk away from my career as a successful critical care nurse? Could I give up the stability of a good salary to take on something so uncertain? I knew the stakes were high, but another thought loomed even larger: **What if I don't try?**

By the time she stepped off the plane, *I had my answer*. I couldn't bear the thought of living a life of regret, always wondering what might have been if I'd been brave enough to take this leap. While I didn't know where the journey would lead, I knew one thing for sure: **I didn't want fear to make my decisions for me.**

The Fork in the Road

I loved working part-time as a critical care nurse specializing in open-heart surgery at a newly established medical center and teaching hospital. It let me balance a career with raising a family. I thrived on the intricate details of my work, where I could focus deeply on one or two patients at a time. My national certification in Critical Care Nursing meant a great deal to me, a testament to dedication and skill and setting me apart in a field I deeply respected.

However, the same determination and focus that made me want to excel in my career also drove me to consider what was best for my children. The decision to homeschool wasn't made lightly or in isolation. My husband, Rob, and I spent many evenings discussing our dreams for our family.

Rob's upbringing gave him a unique perspective. His parents had always encouraged their sons to pursue excellence, even if it meant going against the grain. When Rob was 12, he boldly decided to leave behind other sports and focus entirely on becoming a professional golfer—a highly unusual choice for a boy growing up in a small New England factory town. His family's willingness to embrace and support unconventional paths left a lasting impression on him.

By the time our firstborn was a toddler, Rob and I had made our decision to homeschool. We believed it offered the best opportunity to nurture our children's strengths and instill values aligned with our family's vision. *This decision came with its own set of challenges.* We didn't know any homeschooling families in Massachusetts, especially in 1984. The only two families we knew lived over a thousand miles away.

"It felt like we were waiting to grow into this new lifestyle."

A Family Divided

The challenges of stepping into the unknown deepened later when

Rob's father learned of our decision. Rob's father had grown up in poverty. Education had been the key to his leaving poverty and developing the most successful law practice in town. He had worked tirelessly to ensure his sons had opportunities never available to him, and now, he couldn't fathom why his grandchildren wouldn't be enrolled in the best schools available.

He made his position clear: **homeschooling was untested, risky, and irresponsible.** His disapproval wasn't subtle. He offered to pay for each grandchild's tuition from kindergarten through high school at a prestigious prep school if Rob and I agreed to abandon homeschooling.

For Rob, the situation was agonizing. He had never seen his father so upset, and the tension in their relationship was palpable. Would he be thrown out of the family law practice for defying his father's wishes? Rob and I knew our decision could cost us more than just financial support—*it could strain familial bonds in ways that might not be repairable.*

Our conversations helped us understand the decision wasn't just about education—*it was about what we believed was right for our children.* We weighed our options carefully, prayed for guidance, and ultimately chose to homeschool.

"It was like being tested by fire." I reflected later. "But we came out stronger and more certain than ever that this was the path we were meant to take."

Building Resolve

Though our relationship with Rob's father remained strained for some time, our conviction only deepened as we embraced our new lifestyle. I began exploring ways to teach using what I had on hand. I used Duplo blocks and Golden Step Ahead books from a discount store for arithmetic.

Resources were scarce, and finding guidance was even harder in the days before the Internet. Rob and I often traveled long distances to meet other homeschooling families, *forging connections that became lifelines of support.*

Through it all, our early trial with Rob's father became a foundation for our resolve. "We were tested early, and because of that, we knew we could handle whatever came next."

The Lightbulb Moment

The stakes felt impossibly high. Our decision to homeschool had been met with a wave of opposition from nearly everyone in our lives. Rob's father, who had offered to pay for our children to attend a prestigious private school, was still openly against the idea. His disappointment was heavy. Rob's brother added to it, voicing concerns that our children would never get into college. As Ivy League graduates—a lawyer and a doctor—he and his wife couldn't fathom why Rob and I would take such a "risky" and unconventional path.

While my parents were quieter in their disapproval, their skepticism was no less palpable. Even our pastor was against our decision, questioning our ability to meet our children's academic and spiritual needs without a traditional school environment.

Despite the mounting pressure, I couldn't shake the conviction that *homeschooling was the right choice.* Every time I doubted myself, the question echoed in my mind: **Would I look back one day and wish I had tried?** The thought of living with that regret was more unbearable than the obstacles we faced.

The next challenge was an immense weight pressing down on me. To be sure we covered everything, we bought three separate complete kindergarten curriculums. Soon, we discovered that our son already knew nearly everything about those expensive curriculums. What he didn't know was how to read. How could a bright six-year-old boy with a love for stories struggle so profoundly with reading? While driving, we had listened to *Les Misérables* together. He had no trouble following the story as we discussed it. Watching the three-hour Broadway production was mesmerizing for him, yet he couldn't recognize all the letters in the alphabet. For six months, I tried to teach him how to do it. His three-year-old sister mastered it while he still struggled. I tried to cheer myself up by telling myself, "Six months divided by two kids is three months per child, not too bad!"

I pushed forward, motivated to help my son. I couldn't control opposition from others or the unique challenges my children faced. However, I could control my attitude and determination. We would find a way, even if it meant trying things we'd never considered.

I realized homeschooling wasn't about having all the answers but being willing to search for them. One of those answers was *each child learns at their own pace.* **The parent's job isn't to rush them but to guide them.**

A Vision for the Future

While our resolve was firm, the practicalities of turning our convictions into reality was murky. Then, we learned of a workshop that answered our questions and provided a better picture of what homeschooling could look like. The event, *The Homeschool Workshop* by Gregg Harris, felt like a lifeline.

I took time off work to attend with Rob, who was eager for answers and direction. When the day arrived, the room was buzzing with parents at various stages of their homeschooling journeys—some just starting out, like us, and others with more experience. An air of shared curiosity, hope, and determination felt inspiring and reassuring.

Gregg Harris, an early pioneer in the homeschooling movement, stood at the front of the room and began to speak. His calm confidence and wealth of experience instantly put us at ease. Here was someone who had been walking this path for a few years. He not only understood our questions but had wrestled with them himself. It felt like being with an old friend.

Gregg's message was simple yet profound: **homeschooling wasn't about rigidly recreating the traditional classroom at home.** *It was about embracing the flexibility and freedom to tailor education to a child's unique interests and needs.* He introduced the concept of *Delight Directed Studies*, a philosophy that resonated deeply with us.

The idea was to harness a child's natural curiosity and enthusiasm by making their areas of interest the cornerstone of their education. Math, science, reading, and even history could all be taught through the lens of something already a passion for the child. This approach seemed like a perfect fit for our imaginative and active son.

Gregg didn't just talk about theories; he shared practical tips and personal stories that brought the concepts to life. He painted a vision of what homeschooling could be. It was not a rigid checklist of subjects to be covered but a dynamic, evolving journey where parents and children learned together. His candor and encouragement were exactly what we needed in our search for guidance.

I vividly remember the moment I realized the workshop wasn't just about education but also about mentorship. "Here was someone much further down the road who was willing to share what he'd learned to help mentor us, even if just for a day. That meant everything to us."

Gregg's business was a testament to the very philosophy he preached. He had taken his own journey, filled with questions and uncertainties, and turned it into something that helped countless families find their way. For us, his example became a vision we could adopt and adapt for our family.

We left the workshop energized and full of ideas. The gaps in our understanding had been lessened, and *for the first time, the road ahead didn't feel so daunting.* We had a plan—or at least the beginnings of one—and the confidence to take the next step.

The workshop was transformative for me. I will never forget how much that day meant. "In a time when we were looking for guidance, Gregg Harris gave us exactly what we needed: *vision, practical advice, and the belief that we could do this.*"

Trials, Errors, and Breakthroughs

Gregg Harris had given us a vision and hope. Implementing it was a very different story! The more I tried to plan, teach, and run the home, the more things seemed to fall apart! Time was spent planning lessons that didn't make sense for my son. Tensions would rise from both of us becoming frustrated. Cheerful and chores didn't seem to fit together. I often felt like the house was in shambles, my son's progress was hard to see, and I felt defeated with my confidence shattered. There was also a sense of isolation. *Was hope for success even possible?*

Finding the Path Forward

When we decided to homeschool, the world wasn't yet equipped for families taking such an unconventional path. Libraries held few, if any, resources on the subject. In the late 1980s, there was no internet to scour for tips or tools. Long-distance phone calls—my main connection to the homeschooling families I knew—cost precious money. Because connection was essential, my sister and I would talk for an hour each week, sharing struggles and successes and pooling our ignorance.

In those early days, *The Teaching Home* magazine became a lifeline. Each issue felt like a connection to a larger, unseen community of people walking the same path. I eagerly ordered Mary Pride's books on homeschooling and devoured every word. *This was a mentor,* I thought, *even if we've never met.* Mary's advice became a compass for navigating uncharted waters, offering inspiration, strategies, and encouragement that I desperately needed. Decades later, when I finally met Mary Pride in person, I felt like a groupie meeting someone who was so influential in helping me in my early years.

My intuition led me to reject traditional textbooks. They were too expensive, too complicated, and completely mismatched for my imaginative, active son, who struggled so with reading. I knew that worksheets and rigid lessons would never spark his curiosity or meet him where he was. Knowing what didn't work was only part of the equation—where could I turn for alternatives?

A breakthrough came when I learned of a two-day parents' conference being held a couple of hours away. I eagerly attended with a friend, hungry for answers. It was here I discovered tools and philosophies that would transform my approach to homeschooling.

The conference was packed with insights from experts who challenged traditional education methods. Steve Demme, who would later create the popular Math-U-See program, brought together thought leaders who reshaped how I viewed both learning and teaching.

- Sam Blumenfeld, author of *Is Public Education Necessary?*, offered a critical perspective on traditional schooling, reinforcing why homeschooling was such a viable and empowering choice. Meeting Sam was like meeting a prophet speaking in the wilderness.

- **Bob Doman** of the *National Academy for Child Development* introduced me to strategies that could help my son's learning challenges—practical solutions that addressed his unique needs instead of trying to mold him into a one-size-fits-all learner.

- A presenter on **Charlotte Lockhart's reading program** provided an organized, step-by-step approach to teaching reading, breaking down the process into something I could finally understand.

I devoured every session, furiously taking notes and feeling the first sparks of hope I had in months. *Math that made sense.* Reading strategies I could follow. They provided a deeper understanding of why homeschooling was not just a valid choice but the right choice for my family.

The conference gave me more than just tools. *It gave me connections with other parents.* Some were further along on the homeschooling journey, others, like me, were just beginning. Conversations spilled out of conference rooms into hallways. By the end of the two days, I had formed friendships that would last a lifetime.

I wasn't alone, even though it often felt that way back in my small town. Knowing other families existed, even if they weren't nearby, gave me the courage to keep going.

Yes, homeschooling was daunting. However, I left the conference with a sense of purpose and renewed determination. The journey wouldn't be easy, but who said good things came easily? I was armed with new tools and the knowledge that I wasn't walking this path entirely alone. I finally believed: **We can do this.**

Growth and Transformation

The journey of homeschooling transformed me in ways I never anticipated. What began as a leap of faith, evolved into a profound personal metamorphosis. I realized that while we set out to educate our children, each of us ultimately becomes the student. Each challenge honed new skills within me—patience I didn't know I possessed, creativity in problem-solving, and resilience in the face of adversity. What had seemed like a step into the unknown was really stepping into freedom: by going outside the box, people become more of who they are meant to be.

I learned to let go of the illusion of control. How could I know exactly who or what my children needed to know? I often prayed, "Lord, who do my children need to know, to learn what they need to know to better serve You?" People and opportunities would then present themselves! It created a sense of expectancy as I looked for opportunities to match each child's interests or needs. Focusing on helping my children become teachable led to opportunities where others with knowledge and skills were willing to teach someone interested in learning in their area of passion. *Learning didn't need to be limited to books!* People and experiences, combined with travel outside the familiar, opened up a whole new world. *Obstacles were simply opportunities for growth waiting to be discovered.* This mindset helped create an attitude of adventure as their family navigated the uncertainties of life.

As I connected with other homeschooling families, my passion for mentorship was rekindled.

Remembering how valuable others had been in my homeschool journey,

Rob and I set out to help become those people for other homeschool parents. Sharing my experiences and insights, I began guiding others through their journeys. This venture blossomed into a fulfilling entrepreneurial pursuit, where our personal passion for strengthening families could blossom. Watching moms gain confidence, marriages reconnect, and families thrive brought immense satisfaction. These families weren't perfect. They still had challenges. The change was that they had practical direction and, most of all, hope. I saw that I was no longer just a mother and teacher—*I was helping lead and advocate, empowering others to grow and reclaim roles in their children's lives.*

Three Tips for Your Journey

Through this transformation, three fundamental beliefs crystallized, guiding both my journey and those I helped mentor:

1. **You Cannot Fail:** You are not perfect. However, God has made you the perfect parent for your child. And your child is the perfect child for you. If you do the work, you cannot fail, but if you slough off, you can sure get a D! The challenges you face are opportunities designed specifically for you to grow together. Embrace them with humility, thanksgiving, and grace. You aren't a perfect family, but you are a family working together and accomplishing things that will absolutely amaze the world!

2. **Embrace Vulnerability as Strength:** Your weaknesses are really your greatest assets. Your strengths can become your vulnerabilities as they lead you to pride in your own efforts. Our weaknesses have been given to us by God as his gift to help us trust him. They cause us to drop to our knees and cry, "Help, Lord!" This delights God! He can then show us how he is helping us grow. Acknowledging them and seeking guidance opens the door to profound personal and familial growth.

3. **Release Unrealistic Expectations:** The greatest trap for a mom is

thinking she needs to reproduce school at home. That mindset leads to frustration, exhaustion, and strained relationships. Let go of rigid goals and appreciate the journey and the variables of daily life. Focus on nurturing a healthy mom, healthy marriage, and healthy family rather than checking off boxes trying to reproduce school at home.

These principles transformed our approach to homeschooling and reshaped my entire outlook on life. I grew in compassion, both with myself and others, and discovered a profound sense of purpose. While the path was seldom easy, it led to a place of authenticity and fulfillment that I might never have found otherwise.

The Vision Forward

My journey has now come full circle. My children, whose tiny hands I guided through early lessons, are now thriving adults—each with their own passions, talents, and stories of perseverance. They've navigated college without debt, built careers, and cultivated meaningful lives rooted in the values my husband and I worked so hard to instill.

My work didn't end with my family. What started as a personal mission to educate my children has grown into a calling to empower other parents. Because I personally experienced so many challenges, *I found myself developing a huge heart for parents.* In fact, the homeschool mom is my personal hero: **someone who steps out of their comfort zone to do something for which they have no training because they love their children.** I envision a world where no mother or father feels alone, overwhelmed, or incapable of providing their children with the education they deserve.

My mission is to help parents understand homeschooling isn't about doing everything perfectly—*it's about imperfect parents creating a home where learning thrives, connections deepen, and children launch as successful adults.* It's about helping raise mature children, independent thinkers who are fun to be around.

Every family's story is unique. The fears and doubts I once faced were universal. *What if I'm not enough? What if I fail?* I invite you to see your own reflection in my story—to recognize that the journey to something greater begins with a single step, even if that step feels daunting.

If you've ever felt the tug of wanting something more for your children, I am here to remind you... **you are not alone.** Some people have gone ahead and are willing to help. This is true today, just as it was when I started. **I didn't do it alone!** Whether you're just considering homeschooling or are already deep into the process, there is a path forward. **Think of where you want to end up, and then look for a guide to help you on your journey.**

Julie Caprera

Julie Caprera didn't expect to be a pioneer. In her early years, her Norwegian Lutheran family echoed Lake Wobegon of Garrison Keillor fame. Her father went to work for the Apollo space program, moving the family to Cocoa Beach, FL. Life is bathing suits, T-shirts, and flip-flops when one lives six blocks from the beach. Julie earned her BSN at Florida State University. Being a member of the FSU Student Circus was great therapy during nursing school. Next came 15 years as a critical care nurse. Marrying Rob Caprera brought Julie to Massachusetts, which was quite a culture shock after Florida.

As new parents in the 1980s, Julie and Rob became pioneers in the emerging world of homeschooling. They didn't plan to be so out of the box, but doors kept opening. Life became an adventure of learning opportunities. Pioneers try new things to find the best match. For the Capreras, homeschooling included lots of national and international travel. Julie's search for personal mentors led her to help new homeschooling families. Helping others became the Capreras' passion over the next three decades. Julie and Rob served over two decades on the MassHOPE Board of Directors. Julie was also a regular homeschool conference speaker. An unexpected turn came when Rob's mother moved in with them due to her Alzheimer's. Homeschooling continued as they pioneered multi-generational living. For eight and a half years, Julie served as primary caregiver. A side benefit of homeschooling has been studying art and working in oils and acrylics.

To better mentor more moms, Julie became a student. She then entered the world of online entrepreneurship. A recent out-of-the-box challenge was completing 75 HARD on her first attempt. Connect with Julie at www.CAREhomeschool.com.

Julie Caprera
CARE Homeschool Coaching
Southbridge, MA
Julie@CAREHomeschool.com
www.CAREHomeschool.com

Alisa Cooper

The Journey to Financial Freedom

The sound of crashing waves outside our window had always been soothing. However, tonight, they felt different—more urgent, more foreboding. My husband and I lay in bed working with our laptops on our laps, the aroma of freshly brewed coffee mixing with the saltiness of the sea air that crept in through the cracked window. It was 2006, and we were discussing something that would change our lives forever.

I remember the tension in the air as if it were yesterday. We had both been watching the markets with a growing sense of dread. The housing market was teetering, and whispers of a looming financial crisis were becoming too loud to ignore. The economic crash of 2008 had not yet arrived. However, the signs were ominous. We felt a pressing need to protect ourselves from the potential fallout.

We poured over spreadsheets and financial statements, the soft glow of the laptop screen illuminating our worried faces in the dimly lit room. The scent of fear was almost palpable, mingling with the bitterness of our coffee. It wasn't just about the numbers—it was about our future, our security, and our peace of mind.

"*Alisa, we can't just sit and watch this happen,*" my husband said, his voice steady but his eyes betraying a flicker of anxiety. "*We need to diversify. We need to create multiple streams of income. If the worst happens, we need to be prepared.*"

I nodded, my mind racing. The thought of losing everything was terrifying. We had worked so hard to build our lives, and the idea of it all crumbling away was unbearable. However, amidst the fear, there was a spark of determination. We could do this. We had to do this.

We spent countless nights like this one, mapping out strategies and exploring every possible avenue to safeguard our finances. Real estate, stocks, bonds, and alternative investments—we considered them all. Each decision was made with meticulous care, driven by a mix of fear and hope. We knew that our future depended on these choices.

When the financial crisis of 2008 finally hit, the world seemed to implode around us. Friends and colleagues lost their homes, their savings, and their livelihoods. It was a period marked by despair and uncertainty. Yet, amidst the chaos, we stood firm. Our diversified income streams and carefully crafted financial strategies held strong. While others faced ruin, we remained secure.

At that moment, those decisions in 2006 defined us. They were born out of fear but forged with resilience and foresight. The lessons we learned and the strategies we developed during that time became the foundation upon which we built our financial future—and, ultimately, Tribute Wealth Management.

This journey wasn't just about surviving a crisis. It was about empowering ourselves and, eventually, others. It was about ensuring that no one else would have to face such financial vulnerability again. That night at our kitchen table, with the waves crashing outside and the weight of the world pressing down on us, we found our purpose.

The Dawn of Despair

The gentle hum of our favorite song played in the background, as I sorted through old photographs. Each one was a frozen moment of joy, laughter, and love. My husband's unexpected death had left a void that no amount of time could ever fill. However, as I looked back on our life together, I was reminded of the resilience we had built, unknowingly preparing me for this unimaginable loss.

We met as teenagers, two young dreamers with big plans for the future. Our love story was one of those fairy tales you read about, full of spontaneous adventures and passionate moments. We married others and met later in life. We built a home, not just with bricks and mortar, but with dreams and shared goals.

In those early years of our marriage, we worked hard, investing every penny and making sacrifices, always with an eye on the future. We were pragmatic. However, like many young couples, we believed that the worst could never happen to us. Life was good, and we were invincible—or so we thought.

"Alisa, we need to be prepared for anything," he would say, his eyes serious yet filled with hope. He was the rock, the steady hand guiding us through the turbulent waters of financial planning. His foresight and determination were the driving forces behind our decisions to diversify our income streams and secure our financial future.

Our evenings were filled with discussions about investments, savings, and security. We built a portfolio that included investments the wealthy had used for generations and building businesses that would pay us residually when up and running. Every choice was made with meticulous care. We knew that our future depended on these decisions. We felt a sense of accomplishment, believing we had built a fortress strong enough to withstand any storm.

In 2008, these financial strategies that we put into place served us well. At this time, we had developed two additional businesses outside of the brick-and-mortar business I had when we married. We sacrificed a lot of what we would have considered fun dates out, food at restaurants, coffees, etc., for investments we had committed to place for long-term security. The crash we had heard was coming HIT, and so many lost so much. We were left standing with NOTHING lost. We had proven the investments we made were indeed able to withstand a market crash and/or correction.

Walking Through the Wounds

In the months that followed, we found ourselves leaning heavily on the financial strategies we had put in place. The life insurance, the diversified income streams, and the savings we had diligently built provided a cushion that allowed us to live the life of our dreams. A life we never needed a vacation from. After 2008, we continued to build at least one new business every other year by using tax-free accumulation funds in these wealth strategies.

In 2022, a month after we had planned our final retirement strategy, building out an 18-month calendar to the finality of us traveling the world, working, and playing until we died, the unthinkable happened.

We were on a cruise that we had planned as a part of our reward for the pain and progress we had made during and after the pandemic. We had just finished our time in Amsterdam, Scotland, and Ireland. These were all places that we had never been before. As we were coming into our last port, Liverpool, I found David unconscious in the shower. He had suffered a stroke.

David died five days later after making a full recovery (with the exception of a 10-minute memory gap) due to a doctor's mistake.

Due to these financial strategies, that we put into place in 2006, I was able to grieve without the added worry of financial instability.

During this time of profound loss and reflection, I realized the true value of what we had created. Those strategies were not just about money—they were about security, peace of mind, and the ability to face life's uncertainties confidently. Our foresight had provided me with the means to survive and eventually find my way back to a place of finding myself and my soul's purpose.

As I began rebuilding my life, I felt a growing responsibility to share what I had learned. I knew there were others out there, like me, who needed guidance and support to secure their financial futures. The pain of my husband's death had uncovered a passion within me—a passion to help others achieve financial freedom and stability.

I threw myself into learning everything I could about financial planning and wealth management. I took courses, earned certifications, and surrounded myself with experts in the field. My grief became my fuel, driving me to create something meaningful out of my loss.

In 2024, I joined forces with Tribute Wealth Management, becoming the COO. We are dedicated to helping individuals and families achieve financial stability and peace of mind. The company is a tribute to the CEO's father, who also passed away a year before David, Jeff Miles. Trent, his son, wanted to ensure that no one else would have to face the devastating loss of a loved one without the security of a solid financial plan. He also wanted to create a life without worrying about running out of money.

My journey was not just about surviving a personal tragedy—it was about turning that tragedy into a source of strength and inspiration. Through Tribute Wealth Management, I aimed to empower others to take control of their financial futures, just as my husband and I had done.

Looking back, I see how every decision, every late-night discussion, and every painful moment led me to this path. It was a journey born out of love, loss, and the unwavering belief that we could make a difference. As I lay in bed in 2006, with the waves crashing outside and the weight of the world pressing down on us, I never imagined that those moments would define my soul's purpose.

My husband's legacy lives on through the work we do at Tribute Wealth Management. Each client we help, and each life we touch, is a testament to the power of planning, resilience, and love. As I continue this journey, I carry with me the lessons we learned together, using them to guide others toward a future filled with security, peace, and hope.

Flash of Insight

The market had crashed, leaving devastation in its wake. Friends, neighbors, and colleagues were grappling with financial ruin. Every conversation seemed to be about loss—loss of savings, homes, and security.

One evening, as I was sipping coffee and listening to a podcast, it hit me like a bolt of lightning. The financial strategies that had saved me from devastation could be the lifeline others desperately needed.

I realized then that I couldn't keep this knowledge to myself. People needed to understand the importance of diversifying income streams and planning for the unexpected. It wasn't just about surviving financial crises. It was about empowering individuals to take control of their futures. The thought of so many families struggling while I had the tools to help was unbearable. I knew I had to make a change, to step up and share what I had learned. This was my calling, my passion, and my purpose.

Navigating the Weeds

The path to financial security was far from smooth. While my husband and I had established solid financial strategies, maintaining and expanding them was fraught with challenges and sacrifices. In those early years, our commitment required tough choices, often foregoing immediate wants for our financial future.

One of our first hurdles was the sheer complexity of the financial landscape. Diversifying income streams wasn't straightforward. Investments required constant contributions but were worth the small sacrifice, especially at the beginning. Giving up nights out and daily coffees was straining at first but paid off over time.

Our foray into the stock market was equally daunting. We faced the volatility head-on, experiencing exhilarating highs and gut-wrenching lows. Losing substantial amounts of money tested our resolve and trust in our strategies. Each loss felt like a personal failure, and the stress was almost unbearable.

We also faced the challenge of living more frugally, while friends seemed to enjoy extras without restraints. Investing money budgeted for extras and developing businesses often felt like we were missing out on life's pleasures. This lifestyle required immense discipline and often led to feelings of isolation and sacrifice.

In addition to financial struggles, we encountered countless personal and emotional challenges. Our dedication strained our relationship at times, with arguments, moments of doubt, and heavy burdens. We were passionate, and it showed early on in our marriage.

Through every setback, we learned valuable lessons. Each failure was a stepping stone, teaching us what to avoid and how to adapt. We became more resilient, knowledgeable, and determined. Early successes, though few, gave glimpses of the future we strived for, keeping us motivated.

Looking back, those struggles were invaluable. They shaped our approach to financial planning and reinforced the importance of having a solid strategy. It fueled my passion to help others navigate these waters. Through Tribute Wealth Management, I aimed to share our lessons, strategies, and pitfalls to avoid. My goal was to make the journey to financial security more accessible and successful for everyone. Each client's success story is a testament to the resilience and dedication required to build a secure financial future.

The journey was arduous. However, each challenge brought growth and transformation. I developed resilience and clarity, shifting from mere survival to a deep commitment to our strategies. This mindset stabilized our financial future and brought a profound sense of purpose to my life. With strategies firmly in place, uncertainty and fear were replaced by confidence and clarity.

The true turning point came with an aha moment: realizing these financial strategies were for everyone. This ignited my passion to empower others to take control of their financial destinies.

As I evolved as a person and an entrepreneur, I developed a set of core strategies that I now share with my clients:

Mindset of Commitment

Embrace the long-term commitment to financial strategies. It requires patience and discipline. However, the rewards are immeasurable.

Strategic Clarity

With a solid plan in place, making financial decisions becomes significantly easier. Confidence and clarity replace fear and uncertainty.

Passion for Empowerment

Understand that financial security is achievable for everyone. Sharing knowledge and empowering others is not just a responsibility but a mission that transforms lives.

Through this journey, I've grown into a leader, driven by the desire to make a difference. The lessons I've learned and the strategies I've developed are now the foundation of Tribute Wealth Management. My goal is to guide others through the complexities of financial planning, helping them achieve the security and peace of mind that once seemed out of reach.

The Ultimate Lifestyle

My life now is a testament to the power of strategic financial planning and resilience. I wake up each morning without the weight of financial stress. The freedom I have achieved allows me to live a life that I don't need a vacation from. I spend my days surrounded by the people I love, creating memories and enjoying the peace that comes from knowing that our future is secure. While I will always miss my husband, he gave me a beautiful gift he never intended for me to receive. I will never run out of money. Doesn't matter what the market does, my wealth is secured.

As I reflect on my journey, I am filled with gratitude for the choices we made and the strategies we implemented. Our wisdom and our collective efforts have given me the ultimate gift: financial freedom. This freedom is not just about wealth; it's about the ability to make choices, to live fully, and to embrace each day without fear. I would love for you to take a look at how a personal strategy session could prove to do the same for you.

This story is not just about me. It's about you and the journey you're on.

Perhaps you've felt the same fears and uncertainties that I once did. Maybe you've faced challenges that have made you question your financial future. I understand those feelings because I've lived them. I want you to know that there is a way to transform those fears into confidence and security.

Alisa Cooper

Alisa Cooper joined Trent Miles at Tribute Wealth Management with one mission: to help others take control of their finances and find safety and comfort. With nearly two decades of experience, Alisa is dedicated to empowering and educating clients. She believes in asking questions to understand their short, mid, and long-term goals and then creating strategies to achieve those objectives.

Alisa's return to the finance industry was driven by the death of her husband, David. They always cherished life's experiences and explored the world together. However, his sudden passing forced her to rely on insurance policies they never expected to use so soon. Grateful for the protection those policies provided, Alisa realized the importance of proper financial planning. Her story became a wake-up call for many friends who had never had those difficult conversations.

As a lifestyle strategist for decades, Alisa utilizes various resources, including her life and health license, to assess problems and guide clients. She assists with funding education, making home down payments, planning for retirement, and creating death benefits. Alisa personalizes every interaction, focusing on where clients want to be in 10 years and helping them achieve their personal definitions of happiness.

Alisa's childhood was spent traveling due to her father's Navy service until they settled in Olympia, Washington, where she still resides. She has ties to many parts of the country, with properties in Florida and roots in Texas, often traveling between these states.

In addition to financial services, Alisa owns multiple businesses. Her passion for gymnastics led her to purchase a gym directly out of college. However, she found her true purpose when she bought her second gym, Black Hills Gymnastics. Guided by her mother, a former mortgage company owner, Alisa learned valuable business lessons through experience.

Always seeking self-improvement, Alisa spends her free time training and working out, connecting her physical and mental well-being. She enjoys mentoring friends and acquaintances and helping them find their paths and strategies for their next endeavors. Open about her struggles, Alisa shares her journey of finding peace and passion, constantly adapting to change.

Professionally and personally fulfilled, Alisa aims to continue guiding others. "Though I always keep David with me, it's now about what I can do on my own. I believe I have the power to help others find happiness and a sense of accomplishment," Alisa says. "I feel blessed that this new chapter of my life allows me to help others from both a personal and financial perspective.

Alisa Cooper
Tribute Wealth Management
Irvine, CA
801-644-2345
www.TributeWealthManagement.com

Invitation to Start Your Financial Planning

Imagine a life where you don't have to worry about stock market volatility, inflation, retirement, or how to pay for college for your children and grandchildren. Picture yourself understanding exactly how much you need to save to live your desired lifestyle and having a plan in place for long-term care should you need it someday.

These are the realities that can be achieved with the right strategies and guidance. At Tribute Wealth Management, we are dedicated to helping you navigate these financial complexities and achieve the peace of mind that comes from knowing your future is secure.

I invite you to join me on this journey. Set up a Zoom to find answers to these questions and more. Take the first step towards a life of financial freedom. Discover how our proven strategies can transform your future, and learn more about what the wealthy have known for generations.

www.TributeWealthManagement.com

Diane Murphy

Trailblazing Your Transformation: From Surviving to Thriving!

Have you ever felt like there's a hidden superpower within you, just waiting to be unleashed? It is like you're a superhero in disguise, but somehow, the cape got lost in the whirlwind of everyday life. If that resonates with you, welcome to a journey of self-discovery and empowerment. Life after military service can sometimes feel like piecing together a jigsaw puzzle with missing pieces. Here's the truth: you're not broken or lost. You're on the brink of a new adventure where you get to define success on your terms.

Did you know that women veterans are among the fastest-growing segment of entrepreneurs in the United States? These incredible women, who have bravely served our country, are now channeling their resilience, leadership, and determination into building businesses. Recent statistics show that women veterans are 40% more likely to start their own businesses than their civilian counterparts. It's no wonder—after facing the challenges of military service, these women have developed a unique strength and tenacity that makes them natural entrepreneurs.

As we explore this, let's celebrate these women who are redefining what it means to be a leader and a business owner. Their stories aren't just about overcoming obstacles but about embracing a purpose that inspires others to dream bigger and reach higher. In a world where only 2% of women entrepreneurs reach the million-dollar mark, our women veterans lead the pack, breaking barriers and shattering glass ceilings. Let's discover together how embracing the power of our stories can lead to transformational growth and unparalleled success.

I'm Diane Murphy. I have been on a wondrous ride for most of my life. It was not just during my military service but through every twist and turn that life has thrown at me. I spent ten years in the Navy, forged new paths as a holistic nurse, and have been deeply engaged in remote healing, remote viewing, and tapping into my inner intuitive powers for as long as I can remember. However, my most incredible adventure began after I took off my Navy uniform for the last time in 1989.

Transitioning into civilian life was like stepping into a new world without a map. The confident, take-charge woman I once was seemed to vanish overnight. One day, my mind just... shifted. Suddenly, everything felt upside down, like I was living in a reality that no longer made sense. I lost sight of who I was, what I stood for, and where I was supposed to go next.

Those were some of the most bewildering times of my life. I felt like I was floating in a fog, with pieces of myself drifting away, never to be found again. My brain was on autopilot for three long months, leaving me with endless questions and no clear answers.

Then, something incredible happened. Just when I thought I was completely adrift, a quiet voice inside me began to whisper. It wasn't loud or commanding but gentle and soothing—like an old friend who knows all your secrets and still loves you fiercely. This was my inner guide, my intuitive self—my secret weapon. This voice reminded me of something profound that had been there all along: I wasn't lost. I was simply on a new path I hadn't charted yet. I realized I didn't need all the answers at once, and that was okay. I remembered to trust this voice, leaning into it more each day, focusing on being present and mindful. I started to rebuild my life—not back to what it was, but into something entirely new, stronger, and full of wonder—that was my true purpose.

I know I'm not the only one who's felt this way. Many of us, wise women warriors, leave the military feeling like we've been handed a script in a foreign language. It's confusing, disheartening, and—let's face it—it can feel like you're constantly on the outside looking in.

Here's the truth: You weren't meant to fit into someone else's expectations. You're here to redefine success on your own terms. You're a trailblazer, a maverick, and a true warrior ready to carve out a path that's uniquely yours. Maybe you've ventured into entrepreneurship, driven by dreams of freedom and fulfillment. You imagined the independence of being your own boss, the joy of building something from the ground up, and the pride of seeing your vision come to life. However, then reality hit, and you found yourself facing a road full of unexpected challenges: the late nights, the financial risks, the uncertainty, and the countless setbacks. Your expectations of a smooth, upward trajectory were replaced with a rocky path full of twists and turns you never saw coming.

Sound familiar? You're not alone. Many entrepreneurs start with high hopes and end up feeling overwhelmed by the sheer weight of their dreams. You thought you were prepared for anything. However, navigating this uncharted territory has been more daunting than you ever imagined. Within these challenges lies the opportunity for mastery—mastery that isn't just about succeeding in business but mastering your own life. This is what "Mastery Unleashed" is all about—transforming those unexpected twists into a growth, resilience, and empowerment journey.

Does any of this sound familiar? You planned for a secure future through earnings, investments, or savings, only to face unexpected financial hardships or market downturns. You expected a promotion or raise that didn't come despite all your hard work and dedication. You assumed friendships would stand the test of time but watched as some connections faded or changed. You set high expectations for yourself, striving for goals and milestones, but encountered setbacks or failures. You thought you'd bounce back quickly from an illness or injury but found yourself dealing with complications or a prolonged recovery. You anticipated unconditional support from family during tough times, only to feel let down when it wasn't there. If any of these scenarios sound familiar, know you're not alone.

How do we redefine success and step into our true power as Wise Woman Warrior Trailblazers? Here are some steps that have helped me, and I believe they can help you, too:

Step 1: Develop Self-Awareness

Identifying when a mind story or belief is holding you back and when barriers to success exist within your environment is essential. When you are about to start something, what thoughts enter your mind? Does your inner critic put forward thoughts like *"I am not good enough," "I don't know where to start," "I need to save up the money," "I don't have the time,"* or *"I already have too much to do?"* Does your inner voice support, encourage, and nurture you in moving toward your goal? Does your family or peer group support you, or do their beliefs and fears conflict with yours?

If you're like me, it's a mixture of both. Let's dive into a time when I had to make a decision based on being the dependable one, instead of following my dreams.

I have a history of being the one anyone could depend on. When I was released from the Navy, my partner and I had stable jobs. My dream was to be a chiropractor, and after much discussion, I applied for a chiropractic program and was accepted. As I prepared to start the program, my partner spoke up about how we couldn't afford for me to go to school at this time. He had an opportunity to get into a program he wanted, and his family would provide the money for his education. He applied and was accepted with a start date at the same time as mine. We couldn't both go to school as we had three children to support. I gave up my dream with his promise that he would send me to school after he was done. I continued with my job. Once he had completed his program and was settled in a job using his degree, we couldn't afford for me to stop working.

I chose to put others first. We divorced, and I eventually obtained my doctorate in health administration, not as a chiropractor. My life was changed because I put someone else's dream ahead of mine. However, I made a choice based on my old beliefs—you support your partner. Your partner and family always come first before yourself. Looking back, I don't regret it. He got a career he enjoyed, and I was happy to support him. However, instances like this reminded me that my life training up to this point was all about service, self-sacrifice, and putting others first.

This decision and the beliefs that led me there required a rework. I recognized that I needed to be as important to me as everyone else. I began doing things I enjoyed without guilt, blame, or shame. I declared those feelings and beliefs unwanted and began to pay attention to my words and those of others around me. I laughed whenever I heard the blame, shame, and guilt game. The laughter at the silliness of the beliefs helped me let them go. This led me to the next step.

Step 2: Examine Your Beliefs

Use self-awareness to examine your beliefs and emotions. What triggered them? Do they support or oppose your goal?

This self-examination is a continuous process. As I have nurtured it over time, it has uncovered a lot of automatic reactivity that has no place in my life. I notice things more in my environment. I experience life more. I am more present and aware of my senses. I am living life in the moment.

What does this mean for you? Being more aware of yourself, your actions, your words, or the withholding of actions or words gives you insights into whether or not you are living your dreams or a life designed by others. Let's continue with the saga of me and view another transformational life point.

I have always believed I could depend on myself. I didn't often ask for or allow others to help me. Therefore, life threw me another curveball! I was newly divorced, moved to a new state, started a new job, was diagnosed with cancer while away from home, and now had to figure out how to take care of myself, support myself, take time off to manage my cancer, and continue to work because I didn't have a partner to rely on. Oh yes, since I was newly hired, I didn't have the vacation time to keep getting a salary, while I went through my cancer treatments! Here I was, faced with a terrifying life choice without support in my home, and because I didn't want to bother my family, I initially didn't share my diagnosis with them. My inner critic reminded me that they had their own lives. My hidden self-sabotaging message was that I wasn't important enough to bother them with my needs. That was all inside me because my family constantly supported me. It is a belief developed during childhood as the oldest of seven children, all born within ten years. Does some of this resonate with you? Responsible, dependable, independent, superwoman—I can do this myself!

Well, I did a little mind system reboot and reminded myself to do things that support me, not tear me down. I, therefore, notified my boss and work team about my concerns, and it was amazing to receive! Time was donated to me to allow me to undergo surgery and post-cancer treatments. These beautiful coworkers and bosses stepped into my life, offering support. I felt nurtured and grateful. My heart was joyful, and my gratitude for their compassion nurtured it and helped me see that it was okay to ask for help. The ability to be vulnerable was a strength. The only opposing voice in the bunch was inside my head. It was time to let that low self-esteem inner critic go. With my surgery just a few days away, I notified my family, and my parents flew in to take care of me, further reinforcing that I was worthy and special, not the gloom and doom portrayed by my inner critic. After recognizing your inner critic, negative beliefs, and disruptive chatter, challenge them!

Step 3: Challenge Negative Self-Talk

Notice when a negative mind story shows up. Replace it with an empowering word or phrase. This is an ongoing practice because our inner critic has had years of experience. What are some of those beliefs that stop you? Notice when the negative mind story shows up. Replace it with an empowering word or phrase. For example, if my mind story is, "**I AM NOT GOOD ENOUGH,**" I stop and tell myself, "**I AM ENOUGH!**" I find that laughter at the silliness of these inner stories makes a difference. Stop taking those negative messages into your heart! Open your heart to your childlike innocence and joy, living in the moment. I challenged my inner critic and stood up to her by speaking my truth. I was alone, faced financial challenges, and worried about keeping my job and getting the needed self-care. Doing this allowed me to let go of some of those old stories and build new ones of self-worth. Being strong, independent, and self-reliant are strengths, and there are many others that we often don't acknowledge. Let's now identify and focus on your strengths.

Step 4: Identify and Focus on Your Strengths

Explore your unique strengths, talents, and passions. Notice what brings you joy! When I work with myself and my clients, I ask them to focus on the joy in life and let the other crap go. What makes us want to focus on the gloom, doom, and past negative memories? Why are we wallowing in our traumas, our old emotions? Life is to be savored and enjoyed. Focusing on strengths is not limited to ourselves. If you are a leader with direct reports, are you focusing on their strengths or setting them up for failure by expecting them to do something that is not a strength?

One of my strengths that I hid for a long time is my writing ability. I have many stories and poems that have not been published because I felt I was not good enough, that someone else did it better, that I had nothing of value to offer, and that no one else would care. My most recent metamorphosis is that I am uncovering this strength, which is ability to tell stories. Stories teach us about ourselves and others. Stories are how we learn. Stories are to be shared. If you are curious and want to know more, pick up my book,

Embracing the Warrior Within: A Woman Veteran's Path to Thriving in Civilian Life.

Summary and Conclusion

It's easy to feel like we're drifting without a compass, especially after major transitions like leaving the military. However, remember that this feeling of being lost is often just the beginning of a new path—one we can chart ourselves. By embracing self-awareness, examining and challenging our beliefs, and focusing on our unique strengths, we can transform our lives from survival to thriving success.

As women veterans, we possess incredible resilience and strength. We've faced and overcome challenges most can't even imagine. It is now time to use that strength to create lives full of joy, purpose, and fulfillment. Let's break free from the chains of old beliefs and step boldly into our true power as Wise Woman Warrior Trailblazers. Together, we can redefine what it means to succeed, not just for ourselves but for all who come after us.

Remember, your story matters. Your journey matters. The world needs to hear it.

Diane Murphy

Diane "Dee" Murphy, a Navy veteran, holistic nurse, and author of Embracing the Warrior Within: A Woman Veteran's Path to Thriving in Civilian Life, is deeply committed to serving others. Raised as the eldest of seven siblings, Diane's leadership skills were forged early on, shaping a lifetime of guiding others through challenging transitions. With nearly five decades in nursing and an impressive educational background—BSN, MS Ed, DHA, and HNB-BC—she has always been committed to serving others, blending her medical knowledge with a holistic approach to healing.

After leaving the military, Diane faced challenges many women veterans will recognize. Her journey wasn't just a career transition but a series of life-altering experiences: difficult divorces, losing her business, job loss, a cancer diagnosis, multiple injuries, and a relentless battle with fatigue.

When the traditional path shut its doors, Diane forged her own, working at a psychiatric VA Medical Center to bridge her military and civilian experiences.

Following deep self-reflection, Diane realized she needed to rewrite her story. She opened her heart, changed her mindset, and aligned herself with like-minded partners who helped her rediscover her purpose and joy. She now dedicates her life to helping other women veterans do the same.

As a mentor, Diane plays a crucial role in empowering remarkable women who have served to navigate the chaos of change while reclaiming their strengths and resilience. She teaches self-assessment, reflection, and action as daily practices—tools she used to rebuild her life. Her mission is clear: to guide women veterans in recognizing how their past impacts their present, helping them embrace their true selves, and crafting lives they genuinely love. Diane's work is not just about surviving but thriving and finding joy again.

Diane Murphy
BioSynchrony
Maryland
Info@BioSynchrony.com
https://BioSynchrony.com

Redefine Your Success: Trailblaze Your Transformation!

Are you ready to unleash your inner magic and start living the life you've always dreamed of? Your next chapter is just beginning, and it promises to be extraordinary. Let's embark on this journey together, rediscovering your power, purpose, and the joy of living a life that excites you every single day.

This isn't a one-size-fits-all program that tries to mold you into something you're not. It's about tapping into the extraordinary woman you already are and giving you the tools to shine even brighter. Through intuitive guidance, practical wisdom, and a touch of wonder, we'll help you reconnect with your inner guide—the part of you that knows exactly what you need to be whole, happy, and unapologetically you.

Wise Woman Warrior, download your free checklist to blaze a new trail and redefine success!

www.DianeMurphy.Life/thriving-opt-in-page

Tim Faris

Relationships Are All We Got

Who am I to equip entrepreneurs with relationship skills to elevate their influence and profits? My relationships are falling apart!

This awareness fuels my deep midlife identity crisis. I look back at fifty-two years of success and failure.

How did I end up down here again?

As a child, I avoid Mom's deep, powerful emotions. Adopting Dad's higher rational mind feels safer. This choice leads me into difficult relationship lessons that I'll use to help others.

Looking back, my life's painful valleys occur at ages thirteen, twenty-six, and–not again!–fifty-two.

Safe Living in My Mind

At thirteen, my passion for figuring out relationships begins when I don't say goodbye to Mike and James.

Not long before moving, I practice the piano, then join my best friends at the theater. We're taken on an odyssey "long ago in a galaxy far, far away..." As asteroids whiz past, my mouth opens. But no words come out, and no warm buttered popcorn goes in.

This small-town Iowa mind is blown!

My heart electrifies my skinny body with emotion. What an AWEsome adventure! In 1977, nobody has experienced anything like Star Wars.

Soon, I move far away and never see Mike and James again.

I feel nothing.

"Hey, there's grief in here," warns my soul. "And anger at Dad for moving us."

But my mind's identity story keeps me safe from reality. "No, that's for movies. We build bridges over that negative stuff."

"We need to deal with this."

"No, we always run forward to new adventures... with a positive attitude!"

"Okay. We'll store this to deal with later."

My choice to avoid grief and goodbyes has unintended consequences. In my new school, I'm friendly with everyone but don't say hello to new best friends.

The next thirteen years propel me toward success. I work many jobs and soar over hurdles. In college, my mind thrusts me toward a profitable business and computer career. Meanwhile, creating piano music grounds me.

Summer camp counseling then awakens a love for helping people build relationships. I write a handbook for counselors: *How To Grow Group Relationships*. Curiously, I ensure that campers say goodbye.

I tell my girlfriend, "I love working with people. It's a bigger impact than computers. I'm changing my mind and going to seminary."

"Tim, last year I told my mom you'll be a minister." How'd she know my soul's purpose a year before me?

We marry and move to a galaxy far away in Atlanta, Georgia. There, we attend graduate school and plan for kids someday. My mind's story is "becoming the best minister I can be." However, in a hospital chaplain internship, I'm curious why I don't connect with patients as deeply as I desire.

I try hard, but I'm failing my identity story.

My mind's solution: "Think more. Work harder."

Losing My Mind, Finding My Heart

At twenty-six, I'm unstoppable! Until I walk in the door from a South African educational trip and my wife of three years walks out.

I try to feel nothing. But I'm falling.

Seeking validation and friends in the darkness, I share my story with fellow student ministers. None are helpful. "At least you don't have children," one assures me to avoid his uncomfortable emotions. This begins my quest to learn to be present with people in dark valleys.

Searching for answers in a winter fog, I stumble over questions. While my mind works to appear successful, my heart sinks in grief and failure.

To save me, my soul orders, "Grab the hammer!"

"No," argues my mind. "We're successful because we don't feel that stuff."

"Grab! The! Hammer!" whispers the loudest force I have ever encountered.

My body moves irrationally toward the wall, weapon in hand.

My life shatters.

Sitting in glass shards, our smiling-in-love photo crumpled before me, I sob for hours.

Stuff stored deep for a quarter-century washes out in waves—for days.

My safety bridge lies in rubble. I wander, lost in the valley—for weeks.

While my mind loses control, my soul begins to breathe. My body depresses me for six months, so I can't soar above reality anymore. My broken heart feels everything—for months.

Again, my soul takes me to the piano, where I lose my mind in the moment. Singing "The Rose" repeatedly, my heart cries out in pain about dead winter love and faith seeds blooming through snow. Someday.

One dark spring night, my voice shakes.

What was that?

I sing out deep pain and hope again.

Where did that come from? I've never had a vibrato.

"We've always had a vibrato," my soul whispers, "buried under twenty-six years of stuff. We finally cleared a path to feel it."

Memories flash back to making up my ten-year-old mind. "Dad, I'm gonna quit piano."

"You want to quit? I hear you improve every week. What if you play a little longer? You'll get better and may really like it."

It's curious how quickly I changed my young, determined mind.

Is my soul keeping me connected to what matters down deep?

Experiencing My Heart's Lows and Highs

Summer arrives. Instead of resume-boosting jobs, my soul insists I take an odyssey of discovery. On the Appalachian Trail, my mind hurls me up mountains: six hundred miles in five weeks. With a broken arm!

I'm living my mind's identity story: "I overcome obstacles! Especially emotions!"

After a pay phone stop to hear, "Yes, Tim, the divorce is final," I run through a thunderstorm.

This is dangerous! Why am I doing this?

"Stop!" my soul implores. "We'll break our other arm. We're missing sunsets, people, and ourselves. This isn't who we are!"

Finally conscious of my mind's emotion-avoiding story, I tell myself that I'm a guy who feels and grieves.

This odyssey's next five weeks change my life. I slow to 370 miles, feel every low and high, live in awe of nature, and make friends.

I discover how feeling my heart's low, uncomfortable emotions causes higher awe and joy. Feeling all life's lows and highs is an awesome contrast to my earlier flatline life.

Over the next twenty-six years, my mind rockets me through success and failure. Yet my tireless soul pulls me back to feel my heart, the source of creativity and relationship.

I lead people in churches and as the executive director of camp and retreat centers. My passion is helping organizations and people grow. When I connect with emotion, my speaking moves groups to action, my listening helps struggling people, and my music inspires.

I'm curious how some work relationships can be so draining.

In my personal life, I marry again and eventually adopt two children. Family relationships are challenging and fulfilling. I tell myself, "Family is everything." Years later, family dynamics become difficult. But I work hard to fix it.

The harder I work, the more things fall apart!

By midlife, I'm burned out at work and home.

I once arrive late to meet my district supervisor. He's angry and talks for an hour. I take notes.

I'm proud of my listening skills. Last month, a therapist on my board said, "You listen well, Tim, especially with challenging people."

"You're a terrible listener," my boss interrupts this positive memory. The meeting ends.

My mind enforces my identity story: "I'm a successful leader, husband, and father." But it's not working.

My soul knows reality, but my mind refuses to see it.

Until the job ends and the marriage dissolves.

Wisdom of a Midlife Crisis

At fifty-two, I wander in the dark, feeling everything: grief, loneliness, and failure.

Who am I to equip entrepreneurs with business relationship skills to elevate their influence and profits?

Since my mind's identity story doesn't match reality, my body depresses me again to deal with it.

This "dark night of the soul" is deeper and longer than it was twenty-six years ago. Life has taught me there's no healthy escape. The only way out is through.

My father calls, "Are you thinking about suicide?"

"No, Dad, but I feel why someone would. I have hope. And a mission to help people. Somehow. Someday."

Again, my soul takes me on an odyssey of discovery. I buy a traveling piano and drive up Colorado's Rocky Mountains to heal and question.

Why am I good—and bad—at relationships?

How can I help others avoid relationship pitfalls in business? And at home?

While skiing down awe-inspiring mountains, I descend deep to heal and find wisdom. What can I learn from my challenging relationships? I research relationship skills, brain science, and emotional connection.

Discovering Relationship Frameworks

This quest results in three frameworks for transforming business and personal relationships.

The primary framework is SETS:

- Sensations
- Emotions

- Thoughts
- Stories

Picture these ascending as:
- Body sensations
- Heart emotions
- Head thoughts
- Story bubble above

The goal of relationships is to help others feel understood. Two problems hinder this:

1. We project our SETS onto others, then interpret their experience as ours.
2. We focus on their words/stories and do not connect deeply.

Instead:

1. Be curious and self-aware, separating our SETS from theirs.
2. Respond to their emotions and thoughts (perspectives), so they feel understood.

Let's apply this framework to three situations:

1. Disgruntled Client

Imagine a client saying, "You're not delivering on your promises. My business isn't growing." You quickly have body sensations, emotions, and thoughts, and develop a story interpretation.

We usually respond to their story: "What am I not delivering?" Or respond defensively from our emotions: "Here's how I've delivered what I promised."

Instead, choose to be curious. Respond to their emotions and thoughts: "It seems like you're frustrated with lower business growth than you want."

If you guess their emotions or thoughts wrong, no problem. They'll correct you. When they feel understood, they're ready to problem-solve.

2. Tardy Team Member

Imagine a team member who repeatedly arrives late. Our default is talking from our perspective: "You're arriving late. We need you here on time."

Instead, choose to inquire with curiosity to understand their emotions and thoughts. "I'm concerned if things are alright. You've been arriving late." They may pledge to arrive on time. However, you're curious about what's underneath. "Are things OK?"

If they feel you care and want to understand them, they may express worry about their hospitalized mother. Knowing the real issue, you may temporarily adjust schedules so they can attend morning doctor consults. As a result, they'll likely produce greater results.

3. Upset Supervisor

Remember the supervisor meeting? My unconscious often brings up this memory. However, my "excellent listener" identity justifies me.

Eight years later, I use the SETS framework to understand. Stressed, I had defaulted to childhood coping: living in my head by taking notes.

Instead, what if I were curious and chose to respond to his emotions and thoughts? "It seems you may feel disrespected by my late arrival" or "It seems this situation is frustrating for you."

He'd either agree or correct me. Since I'm trying to understand him, we may connect.

Could his "You don't listen" mean "I don't feel understood?" I could have listened and responded better. After reframing this memory, it rarely returns.

Living Fully and Connecting Deeply

Now, I'm grateful I lost my mind, found my heart, and discovered wisdom.

I live consciously from my soul, curious about what's happening inside and in others. Connected with my emotions, I form deeper relationships.

So... who am I to equip entrepreneurs with business relationship skills to elevate their influence and profits?

One with lessons from difficult relationships in valleys and on mountaintops. Also, frameworks and practices that change mindsets and relationships.

Do you want:

- to connect with clients to elevate your influence and profit?
- to lead your team to greater results?
- your family to light up when you arrive home?

Then, help others feel understood:

1. Be self-aware and stop projecting your SETS onto others.
2. Respond to their emotions and thoughts more than their words.

Let's master this often-neglected, crucial business and life competency.

Because... relationships are all we got.

Tim Faris

Tim Faris, founder of Relationships Are All We Got, is a business relationship coach, transformational speaker, and empathetic guide through life's challenges. For 25 years as an Executive Director of camp and retreat centers and as a pastor, he equipped teams and individuals for authentic, effective relationships.

After early retirement and a mid-life crisis, Tim embarked on a journey to understand what makes relationships thrive at work and at home. Reflecting on personal successes and setbacks, and conducting extensive research, he created proprietary relationship frameworks and learning processes that transform lives and businesses.

Certified as a Life Coach and holding a Master of Divinity degree, Tim draws upon decades of leadership, business administration, and his

"PhD in relationship struggles" to help others strengthen both business and personal connections. His training topics include Creating Impactful Business Relationships, Understanding Your People to Connect, Healing Triggers that Disrupt Relationships, and Building Connections Across Masculine-Feminine Polarities.

Tim also leads the Relationships Are All We Got movement, dedicated to building bridges across tables and around the world. Their "SOUL-ution" to walls that divide is creating relationships with respect, empathy, and empowerment.

An eternal creative, Tim inspires through storytelling and loves playing piano and singing. He even carries a travel piano to play on mountains. He is an adventure-seeking traveler, an Appalachian Trail backpacker, and a persistent skier. In the past four years, he skied 870 days while volunteering to help 340 people learn to ski.

Tim connects with people below surface conversations, aiming for a soul connection. And he equips others to do the same. One of his hobbies is collecting relationship lessons and the stories behind them. What's yours? Tim listens.

Tim Faris
Relationships Are All We Got
Hello@raawg.com
www.TimFaris.com

Elevate Your Impact and Profit by Building Powerful Business Relationships

Do you:

- Have less business impact than you desire?
- Struggle with inconsistent cash flow?
- Wake up drained from troublesome work relationships?

Relating effectively with clients, team, and colleagues is your most crucial business skill.

This resource gives you the first, and most important, step in building powerful business relationships. When others feel understood by you, clients buy your services, team improves results, and colleagues refer.

Because, in business and life... Relationships are all we got.

www.MyRelationshipStuff.com

Mendee Williamson

Embracing Transformation

It was a beautiful spring Saturday afternoon, the kind of day that seemed perfect in every way. The living room was bathed in warm, golden light as my husband, Allen, settled into his favorite recliner. I remember glancing at him, a smile on my face, feeling grateful for the simple pleasures of our family life. However, in the blink of an eye, everything changed.

I was relaxing on the couch when I heard a strange sound—a gasp, almost like a whisper of breath escaping in a rush. I saw Allen slumped in his chair, his face drained of color. My heart leaped into my throat, as I dropped everything and ran to him.

"Allen! Allen, wake up!" I shouted, my voice cracking with panic. He didn't respond. His chest was eerily still.

I called 911, my hands trembling as I tried to explain what was happening. The dispatcher's voice was calm, guiding me through the steps of CPR. "You can do this, Mendee," I told myself, trying to steady my shaking hands. I pressed down on his chest, counting compressions, willing his heart to start beating again.

Our living room, once a place of comfort and joy, had become chaotic and desperate. The children were upset and confused, their faces pale with fear. The minutes stretched endlessly, each one filled with the sound of my labored counting and the rhythmic pressure of my hands against Allen's chest.

Then, as if time itself held its breath, he took one last, shallow gasp. His eyes, once so full of life and love, stared blankly ahead. The paramedics arrived in a flurry of movement, taking over with practiced efficiency. However, deep down, I knew that he was gone.

In the sterile, bright lights of the emergency room, a doctor with a somber expression took me aside. "I'm so sorry," he said gently, his words slicing through the fog of disbelief. "We did everything we could, but he didn't make it."

The world seemed to collapse around me. I looked at my three children, their faces etched with confusion and grief. The reality hit like a tidal wave. Allen was gone, and I was suddenly an unemployed mother of three, our future uncertain and terrifying. My heart shattered into a million pieces, and fear gripped me with a vice-like intensity.

I had no idea how we would survive without him. The man who had been my rock and my partner, was gone. At that moment, amidst the chaos and heartbreak, a new chapter of my life began—one I had never imagined and I felt utterly unprepared for.

As I walked out of the hospital, clutching my children's hands, I knew our lives had changed forever. The beautiful sunny Saturday had turned into the darkest day of my life, setting the stage for a journey I never wanted but had no choice but to undertake.

In high school, I met my sweetheart, Allen, a wonderful Christian man who was everything my father was not. He was kind, patient, and driven by a strong sense of purpose. We married young, still in the throes of college, and began to build a life together.

Allen's unwavering determination and clear sense of direction were infectious. I watched in awe as he set goals and pursued them with relentless passion. He was the first to show me that if you know what you want, you can find a way to get it. His success became a beacon for me, illuminating the path toward a future I had only dreamed of.

We settled into what felt like a fairytale life. Allen excelled in his career, and I relished the role of a stay-at-home mom, raising our three beautiful, smart children. Our eldest, Jessica, was a bright and compassionate young woman preparing to embark on her journey to college. The twins, Amber and Aaron, were bundles of energy and curiosity, always eager to learn and explore.

Our home was filled with love and laughter, a stark contrast to the house of my childhood. I took pride in creating a safe, nurturing environment for my children, ensuring that they would never know the fear and uncertainty I had endured. Allen's achievements inspired me daily, and I learned invaluable lessons from watching him navigate life's challenges with grace and resilience.

However, life threw us an unexpected curveball when Allen contracted COVID-19. The virus hit him hard. While he eventually recovered, the aftereffects lingered. He was never quite the same, often struggling with fatigue and other health issues. Nevertheless, he remained a pillar of strength for our family, never allowing his condition to dampen his spirit.

That fateful Saturday afternoon arrived, shattering our idyllic world. As I sat in the hospital, replaying the events that had led us here, I couldn't help but reflect on our journey. How had we gone from the highs of high school sweethearts to this unimaginable low? The memories flooded back, each one a stepping stone leading to this defining moment.

Growing up, I learned that life can be unpredictable and cruel. However, I also knew that with determination and the right support, you can rise above even the darkest circumstances. Allen had shown me that success was possible, and together, we had built a life that was rich in love and purpose.

As I faced the reality of life without him, I now felt that same old fear creeping back in. I was thrust back into the role of a frightened child, unsure of how to move forward. Despite the pain and uncertainty, a new resolve began to form. I knew I couldn't let my children experience the instability I had known. They needed me to be strong and to guide them through this storm as I had always promised myself I would.

My heart ached with the loss of Allen. However, I knew that his legacy could not end here. The lessons he had taught me about perseverance and about setting goals and achieving them, would become the foundation of my new purpose. I would channel my grief into creating a better future, not just for my children but for others who found themselves adrift in the wake of tragedy.

It was during those darkest hours that I discovered my true calling. I realized that my experiences—the pain of my childhood, the joy of my life with Allen, and the heart-wrenching loss—had uniquely equipped me to help others transform their lives. I could guide them through their storms, helping them find the clarity and confidence they needed to rebuild their lives.

In the days and weeks that followed, I began to lay the groundwork for what would become Mendee Lee Coaching. I immersed myself in learning, drawing from the strength and wisdom Allen had imparted to me. Each step forward was a testament to his influence and a promise to my children that we would find our way through this together.

As I navigated this new path, I was fueled by the desire to ensure that no one else would have to face their darkest moments alone. I wanted to provide the guidance and support that had been so crucial in my journey. Through Mendee Lee Coaching, I would help others embrace transformation, find balance, and create the lives they deserve.

I now see that every experience, every challenge, and every triumph has led me to this point. My past, with all its pain and lessons, has shaped me into the person I am today. Although the journey has been far from easy, it has given me a profound sense of purpose.

As I stand on the threshold of this new chapter, I am filled with hope and determination. I know that I can make a difference, not just for my family but for everyone who seeks a way forward in the aftermath of their defining moments. Together, we will find strength in our struggles and transform our lives in ways we never thought possible.

The days after Allen's death were a blur of worry and fear. Our savings dwindled rapidly, and the reality of providing for my children alone began to set in. I sold cherished items. Each sale a painful reminder of the life that we had built together. Anxiety gnawed at me. I was desperate to find a way to support us.

One evening, a dear friend reached out, sensing my distress. "Mendee, you have a gift," she said. "You're so easy to talk to. Why not start a group for widows?"

At first, the idea seemed impossible. However, as I reflected on it, I remembered my oldest daughter's words: "Mom, you're always there for us with good advice." My mother-in-law had also mentioned that I was a great listener. The pieces began to fit together.

When I finally gathered the courage to start the widow group, something shifted. Seeing the relief and gratitude in the women's eyes as they shared their stories, I felt a spark of purpose ignite within me. I realized that I had a unique gift for helping others navigate their pain. This was the path I was meant to follow. It was time for change—both for me and for the countless others I could help.

The first step on my journey to healing was admitting that I needed help. I started attending grief support groups, where I found solace in sharing my story and listening to others who were grappling with their losses. These groups became a lifeline. I realized that the act of connecting with others in pain was profoundly healing.

Inspired by the support I received, I took a leap of faith and started my widow support group. The response was overwhelming. As I guided these women through their grief, I felt a sense of purpose and fulfillment that I hadn't experienced before. However, I knew that I needed to equip myself with more than just my personal experience to truly make a difference.

I hired a life coach to help me navigate my grief and set new goals for my future. This experience was transformative. My coach helped me see the potential within myself and guided me through the process of setting and achieving my aspirations. Inspired by this journey, I decided to become a life coach myself. I enrolled in a comprehensive course, learning the principles and techniques that would enable me to guide others effectively.

Realizing the profound impact of grief on people's lives, I furthered my education by taking a grief educator course and becoming a certified grief educator. This certification deepened my understanding of the grieving process and equipped me with the tools to support others through their darkest times.

Financial stability was another crucial aspect of my journey. To ensure that I could provide for my family and help others regain control over their finances, I took a financial class and became a certified financial coach. This training allowed me to offer practical, actionable advice to those struggling to manage their finances after a significant loss.

Books became my companions during this time, with titles like Option B by Sheryl Sandberg and Rising Strong by Brené Brown offering insights and strategies for overcoming adversity. I also immersed myself in the works of experts like David Kessler, whose writings on grief and healing became invaluable resources.

Throughout this journey, I relied on my resilience, empathy, and determination. These personal attributes, honed through years of overcoming adversity, empowered me to transform my pain into a source of strength and guidance for others. Each step I took, every certification I earned, and all the knowledge I gained were driven by the belief that if it helped me, it could also help others.

Armed with a wealth of experience, education, and a deep sense of empathy, I am now dedicated to guiding others through their journeys of transformation. My qualifications are not just pieces of paper; they are a testament to my commitment to helping others find their way out of the darkness and into a life of balance, purpose, and fulfillment.

Navigating life as a widow plunged me into a maze of emotions and challenges that I had never anticipated. Grief, like an unpredictable storm, swept over me in waves. Some days, I found myself drowning in sorrow, overwhelmed by the weight of my loss. The absence of my beloved husband left a void in our home—a void that echoed with his laughter and the warmth of his presence.

I was not just grieving for myself; I was grieving for my children, who had lost their father far too soon. As a mother, I had to summon strength that I didn't know I possessed, becoming both the rock and the nurturer for my grieving family. My days were filled with moments of deep sadness and loneliness, longing for my partner, who had been my confidant and my companion for so many years.

The practical challenges compounded my emotional turmoil. Suddenly thrust into the role of a single parent, I struggled to balance the demands of parenting with the need to provide for my family. I faced the harsh reality of job hunting after two decades of dedicating myself to supporting my husband's career and raising our children. My resume, once a source of pride for the roles I played as a stay-at-home mom and community volunteer, now seemed like a relic from another era.

I applied for job after job, only to be met with rejection. Employers cited my lack of recent work experience as a reason for passing me over, leaving me feeling defeated and questioning my worth. The financial strain added to my stress; unexpected expenses like car repairs, college tuition for my children, and home maintenance stretched our budget to its limits.

There were moments when I pleaded with God for relief, begging for a break from the relentless challenges that seemed to pile up without respite. Each setback threatened to unravel the fragile threads of hope I clung to. However, amid the darkness, I found glimmers of light in the women of my grief support group.

Their resilience and strength inspired me. These women, who had faced their unimaginable losses, navigated life's challenges with grace and determination. Their stories became a lifeline, showing me that strength isn't always loud and heroic—it can be found in the quiet courage to face each day, one step at a time.

I learned that progress is not always linear. It's filled with setbacks and failures that test our resolve. It is in these moments of struggle that we discover our true strength. I began to shift my focus from the overwhelming obstacles to the small victories—the daily triumphs that accumulated like pebbles forming a foundation beneath my feet.

Through it all, I discovered the power of community and the necessity of seeking guidance from those who had walked this path before me. These experiences shaped my path and reinforced my commitment to helping others navigate their journeys of loss and transformation. They taught me that while the road may be fraught with challenges, it's also lined with opportunities for growth and healing.

In retrospect, I see that every obstacle I faced, every tear shed, and every setback I overcame has led me closer to where I am today—a compassionate guide and advocate for those who are navigating their storms of grief and transformation.

As I traversed the turbulent landscape of grief and transformation, I embarked on a journey of personal growth and discovery that reshaped not only my life but also my purpose as an entrepreneur. Through relentless perseverance and a commitment to self-improvement, I honed crucial skills and embraced profound mindset shifts that propelled me forward.

Self-awareness became my compass in navigating the complexities of loss and rebuilding. I dedicated time to introspection, journaling, and seeking feedback from trusted mentors and peers. This practice allowed me to uncover hidden strengths, confront limiting beliefs, and gain clarity on my values and aspirations.

The transformation began with a fundamental shift in mindset—from one of despair and helplessness to resilience and possibility. I challenged negative thought patterns and embraced a growth mindset that viewed setbacks as opportunities for learning and growth. This shift empowered me to approach challenges with courage and optimism, knowing that every obstacle was a stepping stone toward personal and professional evolution.

Sustaining change requires intentional action and ongoing commitment. I developed strategies to cultivate habits that supported my well-being and goals. Regular goal-setting, accountability structures, and a supportive community became pillars of my success. Moving forward meant embracing uncertainty with courage, trusting in my abilities, and continually adapting to new circumstances with resilience and grace.

Tips for Your Journey:

1. Self-Awareness & Reflection

Dedicate time each day for self-reflection. Journal your thoughts, feelings, and insights to deepen self-awareness.

2. Mindset Shift

Challenge negative self-talk and embrace a growth mindset. See setbacks as opportunities for growth and learning.

3. Sustaining Change & Moving Forward

Set clear, achievable goals and create accountability systems to track your progress. Surround yourself with a supportive community that encourages and uplifts you.

Through these strategies, I not only survived but thrived amidst adversity. They have guided me in becoming a compassionate coach and mentor, equipped to support others on their journeys of transformation. As I continue to evolve, I am committed to empowering individuals to navigate their challenges with resilience, purpose, and a renewed sense of possibility.

As I now reflect on the journey that brought me here, I marvel at the transformation that has unfolded in my life. The path I walked through, grief and uncertainty, has led me to a place of profound peace and purpose. While I may not be the same person I was before, I have grown into someone I deeply admire—a resilient, compassionate guide committed to helping others navigate their paths of transformation.

Mendee Williamson

Mendee Williamson is a dedicated life coach and grief educator specializing in midlife transformation. After experiencing the devastating loss of her husband at 47, Mendee channeled her pain into purpose, becoming a beacon of hope and guidance for others navigating similar challenges. Drawing from her personal journey of healing and extensive training, she offers compassionate support and practical strategies through her signature program, "Embracing Transformation." As the founder of Mendee Lee Coaching, Mendee combines her expertise with her heartfelt understanding to help clients reclaim their lives, find balance, and move forward with renewed purpose and confidence.

Mendee Williamson
Mendee Lee Coaching
info@mendeeleecoaching.com
MendeeLeeCoaching.com

**Unlock Your Path to Healing:
How Ready Are You For Change?**

Are you a woman who has experienced loss and wonders if you're truly ready to embrace change? Take our insightful quiz to discover your readiness for transformation and healing.

Change can feel daunting, especially after a loss. This quiz will help you assess where you are on your path to healing and provide actionable steps to move forward with confidence and grace.

Ready to take the first step towards renewal? Scan below to begin your journey!

Your journey matters. Let's explore it together.

https://quiz.tryinteract.com/#/66907ea7adcc787aaed68f46

www.ingramcontent.com/pod-product-compliance
Lightning Source LLC
Chambersburg PA
CBHW061259110426
42742CB00012BA/1986